WHAT IT TAKES

WHAT IT TAKES

MORE THAN A CHAMPION

JEFF HOSTETLER
WITH RON HOSTETLER

MULTNOMAH PUBLISHERS

Sisters, Oregon

WHAT IT TAKES
published by Multnomah Publishers, Inc.

© 1997 by Ron Hostetler

Cover photograph by Mickey Elliot
Cover design by Douglas Montague

International Standard Book Number: 1-57673-174-X
Printed in the United States of America

Scripture quotations are from:
The Holy Bible: New International Version (NIV) ©1973, 1984 by
International Bible Society. Used by permission of Zondervan Bible Publishers.

For information:
Multnomah Publishers, Inc., PO Box 1720, Sisters, Oregon 97759

LIBRARY OF CONGRESS CATALOGING-IN-PUBLICATION DATA
Hostetler, Jeff, 1961–
     What it takes/by Jeff Hostetler.
          p. cm.
     ISBN 1-57673-174-X (alk. paper)
     1. Hostetler, Jeff, 1961–   2. Football players--United States--Biography
3. Football players--United States--Conduct of life.   I. Title.
GV939.H64A37   1997
796.332'092--dc21   97-19576
[B]   CIP

97 98 99 00 01 02 03 — 10 9 8 7 6 5 4 3 2 1

To our family:
Dad, Mom, Gloria, Doug, Cheryl, Todd, and Lori.
All for one and one for all.

TABLE OF CONTENTS

ACKNOWLEDGMENTS

Thanks to many who made this book a reality:

To God for the life experiences, giftedness, and inspiration that led to and enabled the writing of this book.

To our wives and families: Vicky, Jason, Justin, and Tyler "D"; and Holly, Janna, Jared, Bekah, and Kensi, who have taught us much about loving, learning, and leading.

To our parents for planting the seeds of hard work and perseverance in our lives so many years ago.

To Charles "T" Jones for his "Tremendous" encouragement and for introducing us, through books, to extraordinary people like Oswald Chambers.

To Jonathon Imbody, our close friend who fanned the flame of this work years ago with his quote of Psalm 102:18, "Let this be written for a future generation, that a people not yet created may praise the LORD."

To the team of outstanding professionals at Questar for sharing a dream and working that dream into reality.

INTRODUCTION

Third and goal. Sprinting out to his right, football firmly in hand, Jeff Hostetler looked for an opening—any opening. But what he encountered was a brutal Chicago Bears defense closing in on him.

It was a spine-chilling moment. Mike Singletary, the notorious All-Pro middle linebacker and headhunter, had set his deadly, laser-like sights on Jeff, while 350-pound tackle William "the Refrigerator" Perry looked to steamroll him from the outside.

What were his options? Pass. Keep the ball and run. Or play dead.

Jeff decided to tuck the football under his arm and run. With one eye on the goal line and the other on the rear ends of his New York Giants offensive linemen, #15 frantically scrambled along the line of scrimmage searching for the smallest opening, one that neither Singletary nor Perry could fit into. Spotting a hairline crack between two of his blockers, the Giants quarterback lunged forward for the goal line. When he opened his eyes, he still had the football clutched under his arm—and he was still breathing. And better yet, he had scored six points for the Giants, putting them ahead for keeps, getting his team into the National Football Conference championship game and eventually the Super Bowl.

I'll always remember that keeper of Jeff's. It was an NFC divisional play-off game in January 1991. I was sitting in the stands with my dad and brothers cheering him on despite the inches of ice we were sitting on during that frigid January day in Giants Stadium.

Watching Jeff that day reminded me of our days playing football in the backyard of our old farmhouse, when Jeff—wearing his ragged cut-offs, worn out shoes, and torn up shirts—would spin and weave and dodge and duck his way around the yard, trying to score a touchdown while avoiding the onslaught of Doug and me, his older brothers.

Hello, everyone! I'm Ron Hostetler, better known as "Jeff's Brother," my new name since Jeff became a star in the National Football League. It used to be the other way around, you know. During our team's "media days" when I was playing for Joe Paterno's Penn State Nittany Lions, Mom and Dad would introduce Jeff—who I could park under my armpit at the time—to the loyal Penn State fans who came out to greet and meet us as, "Ron's little brother, Jeff." I guess he didn't like the label, and now he's gotten even.

As you read this book, I hope you'll bear with me if I sound proud of my little brother. I am! I'm proud of what he has accomplished both on and off the football field. I'm proud of the Super Bowl he won, the academic honors he received, and the community service he performs. More importantly, though, I'm proud of the man Jeff has become and the character he has developed as a result of his unending pursuit of excellence in the face of extreme adversity.

But while I'm proud of Jeff, please don't think I would want to trade places with him. I wouldn't. Oh sure, like many men in our culture, it wouldn't have taken much thought for me to say yes to a career opportunity that offered as much money and prestige as does professional football. But that's not what I'm here for. Most likely, neither are you.

I got my little taste of life in the NFL when I was drafted by the Rams after I finished my career at Penn State. But that stage of my life is over, and Jeff's soon will be, too. Like me, he'll have to move on and do something else with his life.

But in the meantime, I've got a lot of work to do. So do you. And we need to get on with doing what God has called us to do, rather than wasting our lives wishing we could be in somebody else's shoes. And hey, that's the reason for this book.

My goal in writing is to tell you some stories about Jeff. I want to tell you about our lives growing up, about Jeff's athletic career, and about Jeff the man. And I want to do this so you can learn from the lessons he learned, the special challenges he faced, the hardships he endured, the trials and triumphs that came his way.

And why do I want to tell you these stories? To encourage and inspire you as you work your way through your own life. I want to show you that some things in life really do work—if you learn how to work them.

Now, Jeff doesn't like to say a whole lot, except maybe if you get in his face (like I've done over the years). He'd rather let his actions speak for themselves. So what we've done in this book is to put some of his actions into words for you. This way you can see for yourself how and why this knucklehead (as I like to refer to him now and then) worked his way out of his sideline graveyard to the pinnacle of NFL success.

While Jeff may be a famous professional athlete, don't think that he's someone bigger than he is. He isn't and doesn't want to be. Jeff shuns the spotlight and is uncomfortable with people putting him on a pedestal. Like our dad, he'd rather be on a tractor working the fields than working a crowd of admirers. He's just a Pennsylvania farm boy who grew up loving the land, the solitude, and the fruit of satisfaction that comes from putting in a good day's hard work. And now he wants only to fulfill his calling in life as a faithful, humble warrior of God.

Our goal in writing this book is to help you succeed in *your* life's work—whatever that work is—because your work matters to God. And my role as a team player is to help you sharpen your skills so you can accomplish the work God has called you to. I don't have to play the most notable or highest-paid position to do that (and I'm not going to sit around envying someone else's position, either). I'm just happy to be a part of the team God has assembled. I want to be proved faithful when I'm done with the work He's given me. And this is our challenge to you.

You see, it really does take work to succeed in life—there's no way around it. You can't become a victor by sitting on the sidelines, being a spectator. You have to decide to get into the game. You have to roll up your sleeves and get to work if you want to accomplish anything in this world—or more importantly, for God. That's the choice of champions. And it's our challenge to you.

So welcome to the team. And buckle your chin strap—we've got work to do.

CHAPTER ONE

MAKING IT TO THE TOP:
DON'T GIVE UP!

I n four seconds, the biggest game of Jeff Hostetler's life would be over. Just one point and a 47-yard field goal attempt by Buffalo stood between his New York Giants and the world championship of professional football.

As Scott Norwood, the Bills kicker, lined up for the field goal attempt that would determine the winner of Super Bowl XXV, Jeff knew the result was out of his control. He had done all he could. Years of hard work had put him in the position to quarterback his team to the Super Bowl. He had accomplished that, and now all he could do was wait.

Jeff felt a deep sense of fulfillment and peace as he kneeled along the sideline, waiting for the kick that would be seen and heard around the world.

For him, just being in this position to be the winning quarterback in the Super Bowl was an incredible story. In addition to the hard work, Jeff had to learn something about perseverance, about hanging in there when things weren't going the way he thought they should. You see, for six-and-one-half seasons, Jeff had endured the label of "backup." The sound of that label cut Jeff to the bone, because he knew that the longer he stayed a backup, the less chance he had of ever becoming a starting quarterback in the NFL. At times, the situation seemed hopeless.

But now, here he was at the Super Bowl, about to see how the last chapter of this incredible story played out.

A Journey to the Top

It might seem hard to believe now, but if you had asked Jeff just a couple of weeks before the Super Bowl if it were possible for him to start at quarterback in the biggest football game of the year, without hesitation he would have said no. Why? As he once told me, "because things never seemed to work out for me. Somehow, some way, I never seemed to catch a break or get a shot at really showing what I could do."

Those words reminded me of a heartfelt conversation we had one day while driving to West Virginia. Jeff looked out the windshield and pointed out that the entire sky was blue—except for a spot directly above us, where a dark thundercloud hung, blotting out the sun. Jeff's career in the NFL appeared to be headed nowhere at the time and he saw the thundercloud as a direct reflection of his life.

Jeff's career with the New York Giants had just taken a lightning bolt strike that appeared to knock out every kilowatt of hope and confidence he once had. He was discouraged almost to the point of giving up. It was shocking for me to hear him talk about turning the lights out on a game he so loved to play.

Jeff's high-flying quarterbacking career had crash-landed. His scrambling style didn't fit in with the plodding, heavyweight ground game of Giants coach Bill Parcells. So instead of launching aerial displays and last-minute drives, Jeff paced the sidelines with a clipboard, looking more like an accountant than a quarterback as he charted plays for Phil Simms, the Giants starting quarterback.

Like any professional athlete, Jeff wasn't satisfied with merely drawing a paycheck for standing on the sidelines. He wanted to play, and he was willing to do whatever it took to play, to contribute to the team's success.

Finally reaching a point of desperation, Jeff told the Giants coaches that he would be on special teams or play wide receiver—anything—just to get into the game, knowing that the longer he was denied the chance to prove himself, the more the coaches, sportswriters, and fans would doubt that he could play at all in the NFL.

But after spending the first six years of his NFL career barely getting off the sidelines—he played now and then when Simms was injured or in mop-up situations—Jeff's chance finally came.

Finally! A Shot at the Big Time

In the seventh year of his career with the Giants, Jeff's faith, patience, and hard work finally paid off as he was given his shot at quarterbacking the New York Giants due to an injury to Simms. And, ironically, his chance came on a cloudy December day in Giants Stadium, where the Giants were losing to the Buffalo Bills.

Phil went down with a severe ankle injury—one that, as it turned out, ended his season—and Jeff stepped in to finish the game. Although the Giants lost that day, Jeff felt elated at knowing he was going to be "the man," that he'd finally be guiding his team's offense the following week. All his hard work and preparation were about to pay dividends.

The whole week before his big chance, Jeff imagined the plays his team would put together for him against their opponent, the Phoenix Cardinals. He imagined what it was going to be like to be a starting quarterback in the NFL. This was what Jeff had dreamed about since his first year in the NFL, and now it was happening!

Dream turned to reality that week as Jeff led his team to a 20-19 win over the Cardinals. Jeff hit running back Rodney Hampton on an electrifying seventy-eight-yard touchdown play, ran the ball nine times, and completed five of eight passes on first downs alone. He was finally doing in a game what he had worked all those years in practice to do. And it felt incredibly good to be able to move the team up and down the field.

When the clock finally ran out, Jeff was left holding the game ball and a satisfying victory. At last, he dared to believe, he was on his way to success in the National Football League. And he was more than ready for the challenge. He couldn't wait for the playoffs.

Ready for the Postseason

With Simms out for the season, Jeff Hostetler was the man who would lead his Giants into the 1990 NFL playoffs. It was do-or-die time and Jeff had to be ready!

Normally, it spells disaster for a playoff team—even a legitimate Super Bowl contender—when it loses its starting quarterback. After all, the quarterback is the leader, the brains of a team's offense. And it doesn't matter how good the backup is, making a change at that all-important position throws a wrench into what a team is trying to do offensively. But Jeff and the rest of the Giants weren't worried about that. They weren't about to let their chance for a Super Bowl ring slip away. Jeff was confident the Giants could continue their march with him at the helm, and so were his teammates.

Yet Jeff and his teammates seemed to be the *only* ones who entertained notions of success with him at quarterback. Even the hometown New York media seemed to doom him to failure. The *New York Times* tactfully summed up his first four years in the NFL this way: "No pass attempts, no completions, no yards, no percentage, no touchdowns, and no interceptions."

Even Parcells appeared at a loss for optimism, warning the press, "It isn't going to be perfect."

Looking back, it isn't surprising that people saw the Giants' chances as being hurt—or ruined—by the loss of Simms. How often does a team enjoy further success when one of its key players goes down with an injury—especially when his replacement is an unproven player?

But media hype aside, Jeff knew the playoffs were won or lost through actions on the field, not by words in the newspapers. He was bringing to the task before him years of hard work and a determination born of trial. And most of all, Jeff was bringing with him a growing belief that God did indeed have a plan He was fulfilling for his life through what had happened with the Giants.

So the time for talk was over. It was time for the Jeff Hostetler-led Giants to start their march through the National Football Conference playoffs.

A Playoff Steamroller

The Giants surprised—maybe shocked—the naysayers with an astounding 31-3 victory over the Chicago Bears in the first round of the playoffs. They then set their sights on Candlestick Park and the NFC championship game against the seemingly invincible defending Super Bowl champion San Francisco 49ers, who were led by legendary quarterback Joe Montana.

Predictably, the media naysayer articles reappeared, comparing and contrasting the Super Bowl MVP Montana with the inexperienced Jeff Hostetler. It seemed as if most of the media had written off the game as another easy San Francisco conference championship and trip to the Super Bowl. Even John Madden was quoted to the effect that no backup quarterback had ever taken a team to the top before, and it wasn't going to happen now.

But again, Jeff didn't let the comments bother him. He just decided to work hard, prepare the best he could, give the game his best effort, and let the scoreboard write the story.

The NFC championship game was a classic knock-down, drag-out football game. And when it was all over, a nationwide television audience had witnessed what so many people said couldn't be done. Jeff led the Giants on a last-minute drive that set up Matt Bahr's game-winning field goal to beat the 49ers. The New York Giants had earned a trip to "The Show," Super Bowl XXV in Tampa, Florida.

On to Tampa

Jeff and the rest of the Giants had done what most everybody said couldn't be done. They had shaken off the loss of their starting quarterback and earned a shot at the world championship of professional football.

But Jeff and his teammates had believed in themselves all along. They knew that as long as they worked hard and prepared for the game, they had a shot at winning. You see, preparation builds confidence. And because Jeff worked hard to prepare for the chance that finally had arrived, he had no doubt that he could do the job. (He never doubted, really.) It was the opportunity of a lifetime for Jeff and he was ready to take advantage.

Only one more hurdle remained, one more mountain to climb. As the pre-Super Bowl hype began its annual domination of the sports world, Jeff and his teammates set about preparing for their showdown with the American Football Conference champion Buffalo Bills.

Game Day at Last!

Jeff started the day of the Super Bowl with a visit to Mom and Dad and breakfast with his wife, Vicky, and their three boys. It was good for Jeff to see

Mom that day. It was something of a miracle that she could make it, as she had missed the NFC championship game due to a bad illness. It meant a lot to Jeff that she could make it to the Super Bowl because she had once told him, "Your time's coming." That inspired and encouraged Jeff when times were tough, and now it had come true.

When Jeff had to leave, Vicky kissed him and with tears in her eyes said, "I just want things to go well for you." Jeff's usually upbeat and positive wife was showing cautious concern as she saw her husband off for the game of his life. Trying to hide her nervousness, she looked at him and said, "Remember, I love you."

That morning, our brother Doug and I drove Jeff back to his hotel room and helped sneak him past the crowd that had gathered in front of the main doors by having him duck down while we pulled in behind the hotel. All three of us were amused by all the hoopla and Doug and I had fun acting as Jeff's getaway accomplices as we whisked him in and out of secret entrances and exits. One time we even hid him underneath some laundry in a cart and wheeled him through the back kitchen and up the service elevators just to get him to his room without any distractions.

Last-Minute Preparations

You might think that in Jeff's situation, he would be a nervous wreck as he prepared himself that day for the Super Bowl. But as Jeff waited in his hotel room before this game—which would be seen by millions around the world—he felt a remarkable sense of peace and confidence. He knew he could do it. He had prepared himself well and had no doubts about his ability to do the job. He just wanted to take advantage of the opportunity at hand.

After the chapel service and pregame meal, Jeff reviewed his playbook one last time, got on the late bus, and headed from the hotel to Tampa Stadium.

Doug and I and Jeff's boys arrived at the stadium just moments before the Giants bus did. I'll never forget how Jeff's face lit up as he spied his boys standing next to us in the crowd as the team bus pulled up to the locker room just inside the gates. Noticing his expression, we hurriedly picked up the boys and raced over to the bus so they—and we—could see him one last time before the game. They hugged and kissed their daddy goodbye and wished him good luck, like he was a marine going off to war.

Speaking of war, Tampa Stadium was a sight to behold that day. The game took place during the Persian Gulf War and threats of terrorism prompted a heightened level of security. Barbed-wire fencing surrounded the stadium, security guards with metal detectors were stationed everywhere, and helicopters circled overhead. It looked like a war zone and we couldn't help but think of the risk we were taking as we passed through three levels of searches just to get inside to see the game. (Yet that was nothing compared with the risk our men and women were taking overseas fighting the war.)

Once inside the locker room, Jeff had his knee and ankles taped, then got dressed and went out to the field to throw the ball around with Giants tight end Howard Cross, just to check out the field conditions. After that, he went back inside to put on the rest of his uniform and waited for game time.

Before long game officials stepped into the locker room to announce that players had two minutes left before introductions. With that announcement, the nervous silence of the locker room broke into a beehive of restless energy. After the Lord's Prayer and some final words from Coach Parcells, everyone walked toward the tunnel, where they would be introduced to the nation and the world.

What an unforgettable experience for Jeff and for those of us in his family who were present for Super Bowl XXV! Hearing his name being introduced and watching him run out onto the field was an incredible moment filled with pure emotion, gratitude, and pride. For Jeff, it was the moment and feeling every professional athlete dreams of. After all he had been through in his career, here he was—starting in the Super Bowl!

To add to an already charged atmosphere, Whitney Houston belted out a rendition of the national anthem that is still considered a great Super Bowl moment. Everyone was waving small American flags that had been placed on the seat cushions in honor of the men and women who were serving in Operation Desert Storm. Just as Whitney Houston finished, four fighter jets flew overhead, sending the whole crowd—and the television audience—into tears and shivers of pride and patriotism.

With the pregame hype and glitter now history, it was time to get down to business. It was time for the New York Giants and Buffalo Bills to step on the field and prove who was the best team in the National Football League.

Time to Play

Now, Jeff is nothing as a quarterback if he isn't tough. And that was a good thing, because during the first half, a couple of fierce shots from defenders almost knocked him out of the game. On one passing play, Leon Seals, Buffalo's 270-pound defensive end, nearly leveled the life out of him. Even after inhaling smelling salts on the sidelines, Jeff could hardly see straight. And on the next series, All-Pro end Bruce Smith corralled Jeff in the end zone for a two-point safety. Thankfully, Jeff held on to the ball and prevented a Bills touchdown, which, as it turned out, could have given Buffalo the margin of victory.

But Jeff stayed in the game and made some huge plays to lead his team's offense.

Six minutes into the third quarter, the Giants were trailing 12-10 and needed to keep a drive alive. Jeff was looking at a third-and-thirteen and an unyielding Bills defense. It was big-play time. He bent into the huddle and looked into the sweating, determined faces of ten other men who, like him, had come to win.

"Half-right-sixty-two-comeback-dig."

As Jeff leaned over his center, he surveyed the Bills defensive alignment, looking to see if the play he had called would work. Recognizing what the Bills were doing, he knew it would work. The Giants coaches had prepared Jeff for this particular defensive set, and the play Jeff had given in the huddle happened to be the best one they could have called in this situation. All they needed to do was execute it the way they had dozens of times in practice.

Jeff took the snap, pedaled back to pass, and spotted his receiver eight yards upfield. He drilled the ball to wideout Mark Ingram, who caught it and weaved, then spun and dived his way past lunging defenders and the first-down marker. A few plays later, running back Ottis Anderson took a handoff and stormed into the end zone with the go-ahead touchdown to put the Giants ahead 17-12 and within reach of one of the greatest Super Bowl victories of all time.

After a fourth-quarter touchdown put the Bills ahead 19-17, the stage was set for Matt Bahr's clutch field goal that would provide the Giants with a one-point lead. Yet Buffalo still had one last chance, a field goal attempt with just seconds to go.

As the Bills kicker eyed his target, Jeff knelt down on one knee and took it all in. He felt really good about what he and his team had accomplished. He didn't know what Norwood was going to do—miss it or make it. But that was out of his hands. Jeff just resigned himself to the fact that there was nothing more he could do, that he had given it all he could. Nobody could have asked more of him. Jeff had given everything he had. As Dad used to say after a hard-fought game, "You played your heart out, son." Indeed he had, and now it was time to let things happen as they would.

Jeff watched with the rest of the world as the kick sailed high and deep toward the goal posts until it finally dropped to the ground—wide to the right of its target. After one more snap by the Giant offense, it was over. The Giants had won!

Let the Celebration Begin

The Giants broke into celebration, jumping up and down on the field and hugging one another. Several players were wrestling with one another on the sidelines like little kids. Some even got out their video cameras to capture the moment.

In the stands, we joined the Giants fans in celebration. It was pandemonium, an unforgettable experience for all of us. I dropped to my knee in front of my seat and thanked God for my brother's win, then stood and hugged my wife, Holly, to celebrate. Jeff's family and friends shared in his joy.

Back on the field, Jeff was alone with his thoughts as his teammates carried on their celebration. It was done. His stormy trial was over. An overwhelming sense of gratitude and satisfaction—and vindication—filled Jeff's heart. He had done it! He had done what almost everybody said couldn't be done. In just a few weeks, he went from being a "backup" to a Super Bowl starter—and champion.

Postgame Pandemonium

After fighting his way to the dressing room, Jeff had to struggle through the crowd just to get to his locker. ABC wanted him for an interview, so he followed the network people to their cameras. Just then someone asked if he wanted his boys with him. Unaware that ABC was looking for them, but knowing these kids were our passport into the locker room, Doug and I picked up Jason and Justin and told the security officers they were Jeff Hostetler's kids and we had to get them into the locker room. I'll never forget the look on Jeff's face when Doug and I showed up in the locker room with his boys. He should've known we would find a way.

After the interviews, we escorted Jeff outside the locker room to greet Mom and Dad and the rest of our family and friends who had attended the game. We huddled around Jeff in a warm, family embrace, basking in the afterglow of success he wanted to share with us. When it was time to leave, the security people, noticing that we didn't have transportation back to the hotel, got us all a police escort. It took quite a few patrol cars to get us all back. But it was a ride we'll never forget!

And it was just the beginning of a radically changed life for Jeff Hostetler, the starting quarterback for the Super Bowl champion New York Giants.

A Life-Changing Victory

Winning the Super Bowl turned Jeff's world upside down. In the space of just a few weeks, he went from being an unknown backup quarterback to a household name. Everybody wanted to talk to him. The phone rang several times even as Jeff was nursing his wounds with ice while we celebrated in his hotel room right after the game. A couple of television talk show hosts—including Johnny Carson—wanted Jeff to appear on their shows.

Then came the interviews, appearances, and endorsements. Jeff had become a true national celebrity. People from around the world recognized him.

Jeff had become such a national sports hero that he was later honored alongside a man who himself had become a true national hero: General Norman Schwarzkopf, who had led the United States and its allies to victory in the Persian Gulf War. Jeff was honored alongside Schwarzkopf and some other national figures as Fathers of the Year.

Jeff and his family also appeared on *Lifestyles of the Rich and Famous* with Robin Leach, where they showcased Jeff's family's home and their boat and riding horses.

Jeff invited me to join him and Dad at the Evander Holyfield-George Foreman Heavyweight Championship fight in Atlantic City, where we partied with Kevin Costner and ate dinner with Donald Trump at his Trump Plaza. (Dad was really a sight to see in this setting. He wasn't too interested or impressed with all the glitz and glamor. He was just the kind of genuine article that kind of atmosphere needed.)

Washington D.C. also came calling, and Jeff soon found himself on some of its most prestigious party guest lists, including that of the president of the United States. There Jeff sat, at a banquet table in the company of the most powerful man in the free world one evening, discussing the Gulf War—just weeks after most considered him a "nobody."

Super Bowl Lessons

Yes, Jeff had come a long way. And sitting among such distinguished guests at the presidential dinner was a reminder of just how far and incredible the journey had been for this Somerset County farm boy. Somehow, some way, he had been catapulted from a simple two-story, wooden-frame farmhouse in which he grew up at R.D. #1, Hollsopple, Pennsylvania, to 1600 Pennsylvania Avenue and the most recognized residence in the free world—the White House.

Looking at where his career had taken him in such a short time, Jeff couldn't help but reflect on the changes he had seen in his life...particularly the change God had worked in him.

You see, prior to winning the Super Bowl, Jeff had become so busy chasing his goals of a successful career and a perfect family that he hadn't stopped to consider the Lord's game plan. And he hadn't fully realized the ways and means in which God worked in his own life. Instead, Jeff was chasing his own goals, hoping they might somehow coincide with his heavenly Father's.

Like so many of God's children, Jeff had to learn how to rely on God and trust in His plan for life. Jeff has learned that when you are living for God you must have patience and perseverance—and you must be able to make adjustments.

If Jeff understands anything as an NFL quarterback, it's making adjustments. For instance, when Jeff recognizes an opponent's defensive line is overly aggressive, he knows it's ripe for a counter trap. Faked into pursuing a decoy, his opponents triumphantly tackle their man—only to realize the ball carrier has slipped past for a big gain.

Like those linemen faked out by a counter trap, we can charge after our own goals and grab hold of the wrong things in life. Jeff wasn't necessarily pursuing the wrong goals as far as his profession was concerned, but what he needed to realize was that God's goal for him was to "work out" his faith by "working through" the difficulties, while he allowed Jesus Christ to "work in" his nature (see Colossians 3:23, Philippians 1:6 and 2:12, and 1 Corinthians 3:3).

Jeff had to come to the place where he realized that God's path to glory—*His* glory, not Jeff's—was far different than the one he had planned. Jeff had been looking for glory in situational success—a healthy, happy family and a successful football career. God was willing to give him those things, but first He wanted Jeff to learn His own definition of success: To do the best you can, where you're at, with what you've got—all to the glory of God.

That's how Jeff has learned to handle the discouragement and disappointment that has come (and will come again) into his life. He has learned through experience the truth that, "in all things God works for the good of those who love him, who have been called according to his purpose" (Romans 8:28).

Today, as a quarterback in the National Football League, Jeff still works to win. He's a competitor, endowed with a winning work ethic. But he also keeps his eyes on the greater works that God prepared him for in advance.

He keeps his eyes on goals like works of service—helping others whom the world will never notice because they're not fast or glamorous or smart. And he focuses on goals like works of faith—standing his ground, knowing God will help him through difficult and painful times. And he sets his sights on goals like works of love—attitudes and actions that demonstrate compassion, care, and character.

These are examples of the good works God has prepared all of us for in advance. And when you get to the point of pursuing things that really matter—seeking God's glory, not your own—the careers, positions, promotions, and achievements will come as a result of your faithfulness.

Don't Give Up!

Like a faithful farmer daily working his fields, Jeff used the God-given tools of his trade to cultivate a field of dreams. He has learned the importance of faith, perseverance, patience, and hard work in achieving what he has.

But it didn't come easily. Jeff went through the same kinds of frustration and discouragement you may be feeling as you read this.

So what do you do when things don't go as you want them to, when all your hopes and dreams seem to be crashing in around you, when the dark cloud of discouragement blots out what was a shining, growing faith? Where do you turn when life just isn't working out the way you want it to?

When I recall the conversation I had with Jeff when he was feeling so low about his career in the NFL, I'm reminded of Isaiah 49:4, which says, "I have labored to no purpose; I have spent my strength in vain and for nothing. Yet what is due me is in the LORD's hand, and my reward is with my God."

Jeff's six-plus seasons stuck on the sidelines seemed futile and without purpose to his mind. But God had a plan. This time opened up his witness and helped him understand how discouragement and perseverance are such big factors in every believer's life.

Maybe right now you're struggling to reach your own goals. Maybe you're facing what look like insurmountable obstacles, heartaches, setbacks, failures, disappointments, and even disasters in your life. But keep in mind one thing: God has a purpose for these things and in due time He will grant you what you are due. In the meantime, keep working, praying, hoping, and believing for something good to happen.

What works when life doesn't? The answer is simply this: Have faith in God, work hard, do the best you know how to do, and you can make something good happen. And above all, never give up!

CHAPTER TWO

A LEAGUE OF THEIR OWN:

LEARNING THE MEANING OF HARD WORK

Turn left off old Route 601, just beyond its intersection with the 219 bypass, and you'll come to a dirt lane with a street marker that says "Hostetler Road, Home of Jeff Hostetler." It was placed there by township officials in honor of Jeff's outstanding performance in leading his New York Giants to victory in Super Bowl XXV.

These days Jeff lives in his old college stomping ground of Morgantown, West Virginia, during the NFL off-season, but in many ways, Hollsopple, Pennsylvania, is still "home." And the people who still live there are proud of what one of their own has accomplished as a quarterback in the National Football League.

Jeff used to walk that dirt lane to and from our homestead almost daily to catch the bus for school and when he came home from athletic practice. Fashioned by our great grandfather Jacob at the turn of the century, the old dirt lane leads to a simple life in a simple place—the farm. It was there that Jeff grew up, learning firsthand the meaning of hard work.

Jeff went to grade school in Jerome, a stone's throw up the road just beyond the end of our lane. He later attended Conemaugh Township High School in Davidsville, five miles down the new Route 219 bypass. Although Hollsopple was our mailing address, we always told people we were from the Johnstown area, which put us about an hour-and-a-half drive due east of Pittsburgh. (That was during the seventies, so you know we grew up being Steelers fans. Jeff especially wanted to become a quarterback in the pros like

Terry Bradshaw. But everybody knew that the heart and soul of the team was the dreaded "Steel Curtain" defense, and we patterned our backyard football games after it.)

Remembering Tom and Burt

Jeff grew up with three brothers and three sisters—yes, that's seven children—on a 130-acre dairy and poultry farm nestled in the hills of Somerset County. To hear Dad tell it, the farm took a lot of work to develop. And he'll also tell how Tom and Burt were largely responsible for getting much of that work done.

Who were these characters—long-lost relatives from the distant past? Not exactly. Tom and Burt were a team of workhorses. These magnificent draft animals—sixteen hundred pounds of bridled beauty—were harnessed together for the purpose of carving out a living in the rolling countryside. They were definitely in a league of their own when it came to getting things done.

None of us kids ever saw Tom and Burt. They were a part of the farm when Dad was a boy; by the time we arrived on the scene, they were long gone. But those two horses still possess a magical history that comes to life every time we think of them, a history that helps us understand who we are, where we are, and why we are where we are.

We can just picture Dad as a young boy standing behind Tom and Burt, his hands on their leather reins and a determined look in his eye—his commanding voice barking out directions as he focused himself and his team on the task before them.

Dad learned how to work the same way we did—from *his* father. He shouldered a lot of the responsibility for working the farm, even when he was very young. When Grandpa went to market with a truckload of produce to sell, he would give Dad instructions on what needed to be done at home, and Dad would do it.

Over the years, as Dad worked the fields with Tom and Burt, the love of the land worked its way into his heart and soul—and then down into ours.

Ah yes, *the land*. To us, it was sacred and holy ground. The land would outlive all of us. It taught us to be good stewards. As Dad used to say, "If we take good care of the land, it will take care of us." The land taught us the law of the harvest—that you reap what you sow, that the return on your labor will be multiplied like a single kernel of corn multiplies itself once planted and fertilized in the soil.

Tom and Burt still remind us of this stuff. In many respects, they symbolize the values, character, and work ethic Mom and Dad instilled in all seven of us children. We were a tight, competitive family, and we kids were extremely loyal to one another. We fought a lot amongst ourselves, but there was great love and support between us. If someone were foolish enough to mess with any one of us, you could be sure the others would soon show up to help out. These were values Mom and Dad helped instill in us at an early age—not that we would go around getting in fights with the neighbor kids, mind you—that our loyalty and devotion would be to one another. That's the kind of family, the kind of Mom and Dad, we had growing up.

Mom and Dad

Dad was the head of our household, but in many ways, Mom ruled the roost. She was endowed with a more expressive temperament than Dad—probably because she came from a generation of hard-working, rough-cut ancestors who managed to graft some Algonquin Indian into the family tree. (Now you know where Jeff's prominent nose and combative, warrior-like tendencies come from.)

Mom was tenacious in her faith and in her life. Everything Mom did, she did wholeheartedly. That included raising her kids. And if anyone said something negative about her kids, she was all over them like a mama grizzly bear.

Mom was certainly a remarkable woman, and she left her mark on all of us spiritually. One of her greatest desires was that we stay in harmony as a family. For that reason, a top priority for her was family time around the dinner table. She called it "fellowshiping" and we knew better than to even think about getting up from the table until she excused us. All of us kids do the same thing with our own families now.

Mom and Dad had different styles when it came to tending to their children's spiritual upbringing. For instance, Mom worked hard to instill God's

Word in our hearts, while Dad worked hard to quietly live it out. Mom's missionary zeal ran hot through her veins, helping us see and feel the pulse of the Holy Spirit, while Dad applied the realities of working out our faith on a daily, practical level. Mom's nature was to exhort, to constantly remind us of the consequences of sin, while Dad's strong hand delivered the same message in a different way. Mom would wear her heart on her sleeve, while Dad just rolled up his emotional sleeves in a matter-of-fact kind of way.

While their ways of showing love for God were different from one another, there was no mistaking the identical commitment these people had for their Lord and Savior. They instilled that commitment in all of us.

Our parents were also opposites when it came to personal interests: Dad loved sports while Mom loved music. Mom often chided Dad for not encouraging us as much musically as he did athletically.

Mom's dream was that the entire family might sing and travel together, like the von Trapp family in the movie *The Sound Of Music*. But Mom had a hard time getting much cooperation in realizing her dream. In fact, just getting us together to practice could exasperate Mom. She would have to threaten us just to make us stand still, pay attention, and quit horsing around when we sang together. Sometimes she would just get angry, throw down the music, and walk away.

The truth is that Dad and Mom could both sing beautifully. It seemed like their voices were made for each other; they were once the best tenor-soprano duo in the area. They sang to us often and we especially loved listening to them sing, "In the Garden."

Mom made her mark on us spiritually and musically, but when it came to hard work, Dad set the standard. He had a great way of teaching us to live up to that standard, too. When we did, we received praise from our Dad. But when we didn't, he let us know about it, disciplining us with instruction and correction.

Dad didn't have to preach to us about the virtue of hard work—he just set the example. And we followed that example, literally. We followed Dad out the door before sunrise to do our chores while he did his. We followed him to the seat on top of the tractor to learn how to work it. We followed him out to the barn to learn how to milk cows and to the poultry house to learn how to gather, wash, and grade eggs. We followed him out to the fields to learn how to plow, plant, cultivate, and harvest the crops. We followed him as he hauled manure, delivered calves, mixed feed, bought and repaired equipment, studied breeding stock, culled the hens, and treated sick animals.

And when the work was done, we followed him out to the yard after chores to work at our batting, pitching, throwing, and catching—often late into evening darkness. (All the while, we hoped that someday we could have biceps as big as his.)

With such a large family, Mom and Dad must have struggled at times giving each of us the attention we needed without playing favorites. But you know, I think they did a pretty good job for the most part. They made all of their children feel important, significant, and special. We still appreciate that.

They were as proud of us and our accomplishments as we were of them and their character. That meant a lot to our family. Still does.

The Girls

Of the seven kids in the Hostetler family, three of them were about the strongest, toughest, most tenacious young women you'll ever meet. I guess they had to be that way with four farmboy brothers to deal with.

Gloria Dawn was the first out of the blocks, and like all firstborns, she set the pace for the rest of us. The time, attention, and energy she drained from Mom and Dad as she tested their limits caused them to begin pacing themselves for what was to follow.

Gloria worked hard at everything she did without so much as a whimper. Like a champion, she even worked through a bout of rheumatism that attacked her as a child. She still carries a long, surgical scar on her knee, a reminder of the exploratory surgery doctors did to check the extent of damage done within. Her illness slowed her down for a while, but it also toughened her up.

Like Jeff, Gloria was a competitor. And man, was she tough! She could out-jump, out-race, out-smart, out-work, and out-arm wrestle any boy her age. Unfortunately for her, schools back then didn't offer the athletic opportunities for girls that they do now. She could have excelled in any sport.

As our family expanded, Gloria's chores and responsibilities expanded, too. She took on more and more of the work around the house when the younger kids and chronic health problems took more and more of Mom's time and energy. She never complained, though. That just wasn't part of her nature.

On Saturdays, housecleaning days, Gloria would lock the doors and windows to keep us from getting in and trashing the place. It was like a game to us—and all-out war to her. This strong-minded, strong-armed farm girl would go so far as to beat us away with a broom whenever she found us breaking in.

We all remember Gloria as a persevering, competitive, groundbreaking worker. She still is. She's a happily married Connie Sellecca look-alike now parenting two beautiful, gifted kids endowed with similar strong wills and tenacious temperaments. Her husband, Fred, was once a good high school athlete himself.

Gloria is a strong woman, to be sure. But she is also a woman of great faith and has a beautiful, compassionate side. As a counselor for New Day, a nonprofit Christian organization dedicated to serving needy youth and their families, "Glor" has been used in miraculous ways to bring about healing in hurting lives. And she's lived up to her name by bringing glory to God in everything she does.

Gloria has been a great listener and constant source of encouragement to Jeff over the years. Jeff didn't grow up as close to Gloria as he did to the other two sisters because she was almost eight years older than he; she had already left for college when he was still a little guy. But over the years she has been a constant source of encouragement to Jeff with her words, empathy, and spiritual maturity. She has a unique understanding of Jeff's temperament and was able to communicate with him in ways that none of his other siblings could.

Jeff and Gloria are close today and he financially supports the ministry of New Day, endowing a library for it in honor of Mom, who once worked there.

Cheryl Joy was the second coming of Mom—in looks, temperament, and almost every other way. Sandwiched between Doug and Jeff, this middle child learned early in life that things weren't going to be easy or fair. So she created a set of survival skills that would make a downed fighter pilot jealous.

Cheryl loved sleeping in late (when she could) and eating ravioli for breakfast. She was anything but a joy to be around in the morning, especially when there was work to be done and you were in her way.

Cheryl would serve us boys lunch or dinner at the kitchen counter as though she were slopping hogs. (I must admit that we sometimes looked and sounded like pigs as we hunched over our food, all in a line, slurping, burping, and making a mess.)

Jeff and Todd loved giving her a hard time and savored every moment that would cause her grief. Cheryl loved "ruling the roost" and hated it when Jeff challenged her (which he almost always did). His favorite game was to say, "I command you!" to do something she was already doing. She hated that!

Jeff and Cheryl had a classic love/hate relationship and would often brutalize each other with verbal jabs. They seemed to feed off each other's competitiveness. But their relationship changed some when Mom hurt her back and got sick. "Cher" had to become like a mom and care for Jeff and the younger kids. This circumstance seemed to bond Cheryl and Jeff, and they became closer as a result.

Like Gloria, Cheryl was tough—borderline combative—which made her a slugger on the softball field. Like Glor, she could've competed with anyone, anywhere, if only she had been given the opportunities to do so in school. But without the opportunities, she settled on cheerleading, where she performed like a winner.

Cheryl continues to impart her competitive drive in the lives of her three boys and two girls. "No excuses" is her motto when it comes to work and getting it done right.

Cheryl has a strong commitment to the Lord and she continues to support, encourage, and pray for Jeff through everything. It's amazing to see this commitment played out in Cher's family, marriage, kids, and work as a mother, wife, and business partner with husband Steve, a former Penn State football player.

Even though *Lori Jeanne* was Mom and Dad's grand finale, there was no pampering this caboose, the "baby of the family." She would wallop you between the eyes if you ever suggested she had been pampered.

Although I wasn't around much to watch her grow up, pictures are worth a thousand words. Like her older sisters, Lori was an outstanding athlete, but because she went to high school later than her older sisters, she was fortunate enough to have several opportunities to play in school. She stormed into the world and onto the soccer fields and basketball courts like a tornado.

Lori Jeanne worked the English language better than a street fighter and she learned how to play Mom and Dad against one another. One time, though, it backfired on her. Mom had secretly recorded an argument they'd had and when Lori went to Dad looking for some sympathy and a sucker to buy into her plea for recompense, Mom played back the conversation in question. So much for the sympathy scheme.

Although Lori Jeanne doesn't buy it, we older kids say Mom and Dad were easier on her because we wore them down and mellowed them out. But Lori swears it was a disadvantage.

Whatever being the youngest did, it sure made her tougher, stronger, and more determined and competitive in everything she did. She's certainly a great salesman and she loves to win. Today she has a winning personality, a winning husband (Kurt) who used to play college football with Jeff in West Virginia, and—watch out!—three girls exactly like her. The world will never be the same.

The love, loyalty, and warmth that shines from the eye of this storm is beautiful to behold. And Lori and Jeff have a wonderful, beautiful relationship. Their experiences together have forged a caring, supportive bond between them. Jeff would literally die for her, and she for him. And her smile and memories bring instant sunshine to Jeff's face.

Our sisters were and are in a league of their own. All tough-but-tender-hearted farm girls who worked hard, worked smart, and worked to win. Their characters and temperaments and drives were all rooted in the soil of Mom and Dad's work ethic.

Our sisters made a lasting impact on all four of us Hostetler boys and we have never felt more grateful and appreciative of our sisters than we do today. We're so proud of what they've become. There's no better trio of sisters in the world—none more loyal, caring, supportive, or loving. They meant and mean so much to all four of us boys.

The Boys

The Hoss brothers were at one time, according to our relatives, the bane of civilization. Maybe that's a bit strong, but we were a handful. In short, we were trouble—rabble-rousers looking for adventure.

Together we bailed hay, worked the fields, rode the cows, hunted game, broke eggs, chased rats, laughed, swore, spit, and rode the plains of mischief as life on the farm lassoed, hogtied, and branded us all together like cowboys do cattle.

Having one boy like that is tough, but when you have four in one crew, you've got *real* trouble. We later learned that Mom and Dad were seldom asked to come visiting by friends because of us. And Mom, bless her heart, took a lot of heat for "not parenting those boys properly," according to some people. The truth of the matter is that Mom did everything she could to control us, but we battled her every step of the way. Thank God she never gave up or backed away from her responsibilities, including daily doses of the long, wooden paddle.

When her bad back sidelined her, she just prayed and allowed the Lord, our Dad, and our coaches to step in for her and keep us under control. We're sure Mom fell asleep night after night mumbling our names in her prayers to the Lord. It's a good thing, too, because she needed God's help to deal with us.

Third in line from the top of our litter was *Norman Douglas,* born (at least in our eyes) a breed apart from normalcy. "Doug" had a "Dr. Jekyll and Mr. Hyde" kind of personality. Around Mom and Dad he was a model kid. But inside, he was a real politician and a master manipulator.

Doug had a nose for sniffing out goals as well as trouble. Mom and Dad couldn't believe it when Doug was caught carrying out a plot to tomato-bomb a high school teacher's house, or when he got caught stealing a test in class. (In fairness to Doug, it should be explained that he was a bright student who didn't need to resort to stealing answers. He did it on a dare.) Then there was the time when Doug took bets in the high school cafeteria over whether he would eat a fly for lunch. He did. And he enjoyed spending the hard-earned money.

Doug's first homemade corn silk cigarette went up in flames and singed his eyebrows as he puffed away from his hideout in the cornfield. He seemed to enjoy corralling commotion, blaming it on everyone else, and getting away with it. He once started a bench-clearing brawl with an opposing high school baseball team after he "accidentally" gave the catcher an elbow to the chest as he crossed home plate.

Doug knew both how to fight and how to act dumb and innocent when confronted with trouble. He was and is a true salesman and genuine entrepreneur.

Doug was a Clint Eastwood type who could stare down and out-spit anyone or anything. He was cut out for bustin' broncos and slingin' six-shooters. In short, he was branded to outdo anyone or anything that challenged his rawhide roguery. One thing's for sure—we always had to keep both eyes on him as we drifted along the dusty trail of childhood's daily temptations and troubles. Saddle him with a "middle child" syndrome if you want, he had a wonderful cockeyed way about him. Still does. A way of spurring us into spur-of-the-moment adventure, just like Butch and Sundance in the Old West.

An outstanding athlete, Doug resembled a notorious outlaw the way he gunned down his receivers as quarterback for the high school football team. He also had a respectable career with the Penn State Nittany Lions as a quarterback and defensive back.

After college, Doug set about making his mark in the business world. By the age of 33, he had earned membership in the elite top 300 life insurance underwriters in the nation. Today, he is a certified financial planner and a principal of Hostetler and Associates, LLC. He recently contributed to writing a book titled *Wealth Enhancement & Preservation* and specializes in pension plan design, business continuation and estate planning, insurance benefits, and investment portfolio management. His interests have certainly influenced Jeff, who also became a certified financial planner. Years of hard work and business success now afford Doug financial independence and the goal he cherishes most—time with his own family.

Doug has accomplished his success by setting goals and pursuing them. He says he started making goals at the age of ten. As he got older he would set sports goals—to be stronger, faster, or just better. When he talks about that now, he still can't put into words why he is like that. Maybe it's because he had brothers to compete with. Or maybe it had something to do with the affirmation and encouragement he'd get from Mom and Dad, especially when Dad played with him.

Besides finding an athletic cheerleader and beautiful, artistic wife to marry—which he did in Nancy—Doug's ambitions also included spiritual goals. He was saved at the age of twelve at a Billy Graham crusade and right away he started memorizing all the Bible verses Billy Graham suggested at the crusade—verses on the assurance of salvation and a gospel presentation.

Much like Dad, Doug didn't necessarily have to enjoy a task to see it to its completion. To those two it was just a matter of discipline. That's something I'm sure Doug's three boys and daughter will learn, too.

Jon Todd, our youngest brother, faced the unenviable task of following three successful brothers. While he personally felt confident in establishing his own credentials, others seemed bent on comparisons. But Todd was more than happy to take his own path in life and not worry about the comparisons.

He took one of those paths when Penn State football coach Joe Paterno declined to offer him a scholarship to play for the Nittany Lions. Some guys might be upset that they couldn't follow in their brothers' footsteps, but not Todd. Instead of playing football at another school (he was offered other scholarships from Division I colleges), Todd took up a baseball scholarship instead…at Penn State. And he excelled.

Athletically, Todd was much more than a chip off the old block—he was the whole block reproduced. A lot of guys can say, "Thanks, Dad!" for the family yacht or ocean frontage in South Florida, but Todd can say thanks to our dad for a more important legacy: He loves the game of baseball. Todd came to a love of baseball on his own, too, because Dad never forced it on him. Todd was a natural, ripping and catching the ball like Norman Jr. himself. I guess you could say his ability in baseball was genetic, except for one detail: Todd batted left-handed, while Dad was a right-handed hitter.

Today Todd is carving out his own niche of success as a financial planner. He has launched a profitable and growing consulting enterprise in Columbia, Maryland.

Although an accident cut short Todd's baseball career (Todd was a pro baseball prospect until he was struck by a car one dark, rainy night on the Penn State campus. The accident fractured his leg and his skull and nearly killed him. He recovered, but the accident caused him to lose some foot speed and ruined his baseball swing), don't think for a moment that he has been shortchanged on competitive drive. Like all his siblings, Todd is a hardworking, competitive person. And you can be sure he will deed this characteristic to his two sons and daughter along with the help of his wife, Lisa, who was quite a star on the college tennis court.

Memories and Lessons on the Farm

Although the sign at the end of the lane back home is still there, Mom and Dad aren't. Dad retired from farming after Mom died in 1991. After that, Jeff bought the farm and then gave it to the Mennonite Foundation. Today, that old two-story farmhouse is home to a Mennonite family who operates the old farm just like our family did for so many years.

The farmhouse and the land are no longer a part of the Hostetler family. If you were to visit there today, we'd be gone. So would the old barn that was destroyed by fire years back. So would Tom and Burt.

For us, the days of slopping hogs, milking cows, hauling manure, bailing hay, gathering eggs, picking peas, canning corn, and selling milk are long gone. So are the days of walking the dirt lane, making tunnels in the hay mow, and doing donuts in the fields with the old Ford truck.

But for Jeff and for all of us, the memories of the farm live on. So do the lessons we learned and the values our parents engraved on our characters as we worked to make a living. Although the farm's landscape and tenants have changed, the memories remain of a distant time and a different place. It's a time and place that passed on to us the rock-solid, time-tested, enduring values that we still hold so dear, values like a solid work ethic, allegiance to duty, loyalty, fear of God, respect for authority, teamwork, self-restraint, perseverance and, yes, character.

Jeff is grateful for the influence Mom and Dad, brothers and sisters, and even Tom and Burt have had in his life. And he's thankful for the values he and his family learned on the farm. These are the values he works so hard to instill in his three boys.

Jeff understands that the families who win are the families who know how to collar their energies and resources in a particular direction and for a specific purpose. He knows the benefits go to those who are better trained, better conditioned, better prepared, better matched, and better utilized.

Above all, Jeff knows how vital it is to have his heavenly Father in control of his family. "God has to be at the center of our families," he says, "and we've got to love each other unconditionally as family members. It's one thing to hear about what we're supposed to do and another thing to see it lived out. Thankfully, I had the rare privilege of seeing it lived out in our family. We were far from perfect, but at the core of our family was a solid faith in God and a real, honest love for each other."

These are some of the things that we learned on the family farm. And, of course, we learned the value of hard work.

Hard Work Brings Enduring Benefits

Sadly, we live in a time when survey after survey reveals that fewer and fewer Americans want to work hard or take pride in what they do; when families no longer value a strong work ethic; when young people live for the moment rather than working patiently toward a future. We live in a society of people who want white-collar rewards without a blue-collar work ethic, who want the win without the wait, the prize without the pull, and the character without the work.

How do you suppose we got to this point? It's easy to blame our society's rampant materialism for these attitudes. People want what they want, and they want it now.

We didn't have time for those kinds of attitudes back on the farm. At the end of the dirt lane back home, we didn't have much. We didn't have VCRs, CD players, or personal computer games competing for our time. We didn't wear the latest fashions, live in the classiest neighborhood, or drive the most expensive cars. We seldom ate out or received much if any allowance.

We didn't have the newest sports equipment to play with, either. We used coat hangers for basketball rims and tattered Wiffle balls to shoot with. We played on a gravel and dirt "floor" and used the side of the chicken house for a backboard. We didn't have breakaway rims, macadam playing surfaces, or "Air Jordans" to slip into. When the weather got bad, we built our own indoor sports coliseum inside the metal grain bin, stringing up a few lights in order to play at night after chores. And even though the protruding nuts and bolts tore up our knuckles and skinned our shoulders on our driving lay-ups, we healed.

We rarely took vacations or days off from our chores, even when we were sick. We worked seven days a week, including holidays. The only time off we got were minivacations in the form of Sunday afternoon naps after church.

On the outside it didn't look like we had much on the old Hostetler farm. But you're wrong if you think we sat around feeling sorry for ourselves. We didn't have time for that. Besides, Mom and Dad wouldn't allow it. They understood the principle, "necessity is the mother of invention." So they engaged us with chores needing to be done, problems to solve, and difficulties to fix. Their way led to growth, helped our self-confidence, added to our significance, generated a feeling of security, and enhanced the meaning of family by strengthening our relationships with one another.

All of these things were a product of an enterprising mix of imagination, invention, creation, and engineering.

So what's my point? It's simple. If Jeff had been more concerned about what he didn't have than what he did have, I don't think he would have acquired the kind of character—the kind of work ethic—that helped get him to the Super Bowl. And he certainly wouldn't have gained the kind of character that has made him the husband, the father, and the man of God he is today.

Without that character, Jeff would have quit when things got tough. When something didn't go his way, he would have made excuses, blamed other people, or used his energy and talents in the pursuit of things that didn't matter. He would have dropped out of school, dropped his family, dropped sports, dropped church, and dropped out of life.

But he didn't do that. When life threw him a curve (and we'll talk about a few of them shortly), Jeff didn't become bitter. He got better! Instead of worrying about what he didn't have, Jeff worked on developing the things he did have. And he continued to work and remind himself of God's plan for his life.

That is what we Pennsylvanians call "the Mennonite work ethic." It's simple, really. It just means that you don't quit. When you're down, you continue to work hard, knowing that somehow God's going to get you through the tough times.

It is this kind of character which has helped Jeff grow stronger in mind, body, and spirit, even through the worst of the trials. And it is this kind of faithful preparation that carried over to his NFL career and catapulted him toward a Super Bowl victory. How could Jeff fail to thank God for what he learned on the farm? It has helped him live out his dreams, fulfilling dreams which grew out of the fertile soil of what is called a work ethic.

It's a simple lesson, really, but one we all need to learn. If we want to succeed, it takes work! Jeff Hostetler learned this lesson from the simple folks who lived it daily on a farm at the end of a dirt lane just off old Route 601.

CHAPTER THREE

THE CHOICE OF CHAMPIONS:
A HEART FOR COMPETITION

The time was now or never. It was up to Jeff to take possession of first place and the championship, while the former champion and current leader of the pack, Dan Marino, looked on.

Welcome to the 1993 NFL Quarterback Challenge at the Walt Disney World Resort in Orlando, Florida, where the very best in the National Football League put their pride and skills on display in an exhibition of quarterbacking skills. Competing in this year's event were Troy Aikman, Steve Young, Dan Marino, Jim Harbaugh, Jim Everett, Randall Cunningham, Boomer Esiason, Jim Kelly, Warren Moon, and Jeff.

The contest consisted of four events: the "Accuracy Shoot-Out;" "Speed & Mobility;" "Distance Throw;" and "Read & Recognition."

Steve Young won the Accuracy Shoot-Out, which resembled an archery contest. The goal was to score as many points as possible by hitting the bull's-eye on a close-range target. Next came the Speed and Mobility event, where each player got two throws at a still target from close range...while running an obstacle course. The goal was to run the course as fast as possible while making an accurate throw. Aikman barely edged out Jeff for the win.

Although Jeff hadn't won either of the first two events, his combined score totaled seventy-seven points, placing him second to Aikman, with the Distance Throw coming up. In this event, each player was given two long throws to determine who had the strongest arm. The ball had to land between hash marks, with two points awarded for every yard over 40.

Cunningham won the event while Jeff came in fourth.

With only one event left in the Quarterback Challenge, Jeff was leading the standings with a total of 119 points, four more than Aikman and Young. Things were really beginning to heat up as each player prepared for the final and most important event, the Read & Recognition. This event accounted for 51 percent of the participant's final score, which made it possible for a player to come from way behind and win the title.

In the Read & Recognition, each player got four throws to hit one of five targets located at various positions on the field. Some of the targets moved across the field while the others remained stationary. More points were given for hitting the "live" and deepest targets than the closer, stationary ones. The tip of the ball was chalked to mark each hit on the target.

Moon jumped out front with some dramatic throws which accumulated some big points. Esiason followed with two good throws, but was forced to throw deep on his last two to try to catch Moon. Marino then stepped up to attempt a comeback. His first two throws scored big. After his third throw he politicked the judges for a favorable spot and some extra points, which he got. He took the lead on his final toss, hoping it was enough to help him land his third straight Quarterback Challenge victory.

With everyone eliminated but Jeff, Marino appeared to be on his way to another win.

But Hoss wasn't about to let that happen.

Jeff needed seventy-seven points and an outstanding four throws to win. On his first throw he rifled a bull's-eye for 36 points.

With a smile on his face, his hand on the football, and fans in the stands cheering him on, Jeff dropped back for his second throw. The crowd roared as Jeff launched another pass that struck the heart of the target. Jeff turned and smiled at Marino while Dan just shook his head in disbelief. In two throws, Jeff earned 72 points, leaving him just five points shy of passing Marino and taking the title. On his third throw Jeff nailed the final target to come from behind and win the 1993 NFL Quarterback Challenge.

A Passion for Winning

You'll never see the results of the Quarterback Challenge on the front page of your local newspaper's sports section, and it will never make the highlights of ESPN's NFL Prime Time. The Quarterback Challenge is supposed to be a fun made-for-TV event where everybody gets together, shows off their athletic ability, and has a few laughs. It's not supposed to be serious.

Well, just try telling that to the guys who compete. In truth, each of the participants in the Quarterback Challenge knows he is competing directly with the best in the business, and each of these men wants to win.

When you think about it, that's a lot of what makes a quarterback great. It's the competitiveness, the driving will to win. Since the creation of football, all the great quarterbacks had a passion to be the best on the field on any given day, to do everything within their power to win.

Jeff Hostetler is no exception to that rule. Anyone who saw Jeff lead his New York Giants football team to victory in Super Bowl XXV had to admire his unyielding courage, his rawhide toughness, and his determined competitiveness.

When 270-pound Buffalo Bills defensive end Leon Seals body-slammed him into semiconsciousness, viewers from around the world assumed Jeff was down for the count. But Jeff picked himself up and on the very next series he punched a pinpoint pass into the end zone to help lead the Giants to the win over the Bills.

That kind of performance is typical of Jeff Hostetler, the NFL quarterback. While he may not have Hall-of-Fame statistics, he wins with determination, toughness, and competitiveness.

Some might think that side of Jeff's personality seems incongruous with his otherwise retiring personality, leading them to wonder, *Where does his incredible fighting spirit come from?*

Well, you might say he came by it naturally.

Weighing in at a little over eleven pounds, William Jeffrey Hostetler entered the competitive arena of life on April 22, 1961, capable of pancaking two-year-old toddlers—not with left jabs or right hooks, but with size. As a baby, he looked something like Jabba the Hutt in the movie *Return of the Jedi*. Early on, because he was so big and his legs couldn't yet support his weight, he mastered the "fireman's slide"—just stop, drop, and roll.

Homemade Competition

Jeff's competitiveness can also be traced to our home on the chicken and dairy farm, where he grew up with three brothers and three sisters—each of them as competitive and tough as the next. That's more than enough to nurture anybody's competitive drive.

Competition was a big part of our lives on the farm; we competed at everything! The first contests we can remember were focused on gathering eggs in the chicken house. Todd and Jeff would sit on the bottom shelf of the egg carts piloted by Doug and me, gathering eggs on the lower level while we gathered the top rows. We raced to see who could get done first, with one rule: If Todd and Jeff missed any eggs, we would make them go back later and gather them by themselves.

We competed at almost anything and everything we did—from hauling manure to washing and grading eggs to schoolwork to sports. The competition was great motivation because it made us all work harder at whatever we did.

Perhaps the competition had as much to do with getting and receiving attention from Mom and Dad as it did with actually beating one another. After all, getting noticed and being affirmed and recognized in such a large family was a challenge, even if our parents never compared us with one another or goaded us to compete with one another.

A good example of this: schoolwork. Dad and Mom always placed high priority on academics. Dad always said he wanted us to get good grades and go on and do something with our lives, so that we wouldn't have to eke out a living like he had to. That confused us, in a way, because we always admired Dad for the work he did. We truly looked up to him for the way he provided for us.

Nevertheless, we all worked hard in school and got good grades. We competed with one another in who could bring home the better marks. We never received any money or other material rewards for good scholastic performances, but we did receive praise and recognition from Mom and Dad, and that meant a lot to each of us. Each of us also knew we would never hear the end of it from our brothers and sisters if their grades were better than ours.

Dad — A Model of Competitiveness

If we kids needed an example of how to be competitive, we needed look no further than Dad. He wasn't just an excellent father figure, but a great athlete, sportsman, and farmer. Dad was very competitive and worked hard to do his best in everything.

Standing only five feet nine inches tall, Dad still played big on the softball field. He could charge a bunt down the third base line, scoop it up, and sidearm it to first on a rope before the batter was even out of the box. And Dad was always willing to sacrifice himself upon the altar of the infield when he played. I remember one day after his team won a softball tournament we asked him why he didn't receive the MVP award. In our eyes, nobody came close to performing the way he did or played such a significant role. Undaunted, he said, "Here's my trophy," showing us the big, red burn tattooed on his hip. We got the message.

Dad's competitive fire didn't just burn on the softball field; it also played a big part in one of his passions: hunting. When it came to tracking deer, Dad was "The Man." Everyone called him the "Great White Hunter." He seemed to have a special sense for it. Although a lifetime of working around loud farm machinery eventually got the best of his hearing, he could smell a whitetail miles away.

We still laugh when we recall the time Todd and Jeff first went hunting with Dad. They were out well before daylight and by the time dawn broke, Todd and Jeff were tired, sleepy, hungry, and freezing. The hike into the woods was more like a military march than a fun-loving excursion, and before long Dad was carrying Todd's and Jeff's rifles and coats (and maybe Todd and Jeff themselves) through the mountain laurel, across slab piles, over the choppings and fallen timber, and up the road to a good spot on the

side of the mountain. Then, after positioning Jeff several yards away but keeping Todd with him, they waited, hoping for some action.

On this particular occasion the action came and went before either Todd or Jeff saw it. Halfway through his midmorning apple, Dad paused to check the wind and that specially developed sense that told him when a deer was nearby. Something *was* in the air. The look on Dad's face said so, despite the sliver of apple peel dangling from his motionless lower lip. In the blink of an eye, he had his gun raised, sights set, crosshairs focused, and trigger finger ready to squeeze off a shot before the rest of the apple hit the ground. He had spotted a set of antlers no one else could see.

He paused for a moment, resisting the temptation to pull his ever-itching trigger finger in order to give Todd the first crack. Problem was, Todd wasn't ready. He couldn't see or hear a deer anywhere, let alone a multipronged buck. And while he squinted and squirmed to find a deer and some antlers to go with it, Dad quietly whispered, "Take him, Jonnie, take him."

But you can't shoot what you can't see, and while the seconds passed, so did the deer. In a matter of moments it disappeared into the brush like a silent ghost, spooked by the scent of father and sons. So it seemed to Todd and Jeff, anyway.

The deer wasn't gone, however. And no distance was beyond the eye of the Master. You have to know how to shoot to compete with this deer slayer. Show Dad so much as a whisker, and he'll find it and remove it at any range. Just when his frustrated and bewildered sons lowered their rifles in despair, Dad swung his rifle around in one magnificent motion and squeezed off a thunderous shot. And with a smile that said "nothin' but net" he looked over to Todd and said, "I think I got him, Jonnie."

Well, of course he did.

In heavy brush and far enough away to qualify for a long-distance phone call, they found his buck. Dad had slam dunked another trophy. The incident has remained frozen in Todd and Jeff's competitive quiver to this day. Dad's love for hunting was passed on to Jeff, who has bagged his share of deer. I can still remember the doe Jeff picked off while it was standing in a herd up by the "round woods" back home on the farm. Dad spied some deer eating his corn and came into the house to get his rifle (and us). He wanted to see who could get 'em from our perch next to the shed out back, at least eight football fields away.

I don't recall who shot first, but whoever it was he missed, causing the herd to scatter a few steps. But because we were so far away and the deer didn't know we were shooting at them, they didn't run off. Jeff went next, and after he pulled the trigger, one of the deer seemed to fall, although the herd never moved. After another shot, however, the herd ran off and Jeff said "I think I got him." We didn't believe it (or even want to believe it) so we hurriedly hiked up toward where the herd had been to check it out. Although we couldn't find a mark on it, the deer lay there, dead as a doornail. And while Jeff celebrated, we reluctantly acknowledged his championship shot.

Dad's competitiveness also made itself known in his life as a farmer. Call it competitiveness or call it hard work, Dad was a practitioner of the Mennonite work ethic, which states that you don't quit, no matter how tough the going gets. It means that when you're down, you keep working hard, knowing that God will get you through the tough times.

One of those tough times is still etched in memory. It was the time our barn burned down, taking years of hard work with it.

It was a hot summer night and Mom came racing through the house, shouting, "Kids! Wake up! The barn's burning! The barn's burning!" We awoke to the yellow glow of the blaze and the cracking sound of burning timbers. We knew something dreadful was happening.

We all watched in horror as our barn burned to the ground. Mom called the fire company while Dad and I, crouched beneath a water-soaked blanket to ward off the heat, pulled our dog to safety through a hole in the side of the barn, just before timbers crashed down.

It was a total loss; only half its value had been insured. To make matters worse, our harvest of hay had just been bailed and stored in the barn, thanks to the help of our Mennonite neighbors.

Just weeks before the fire, Dad had been laid up with what the doctors initially suspected was a brain tumor. All the tests for a tumor turned out negative, though, and it turned out Dad had caught a rare flu virus sweeping the area. The flu caused Dad to mysteriously lose his strength and sense of balance. Once he slipped into the gutter in the barn and another time he fell to the ground trying to climb up on the tractor. He tried to play ball one night and fell down flat on his face and broke his thumb. This wasn't the mighty ballplayer and hunter we knew.

Our neighbors pitched in to harvest our hay and stack it all in the barn, despite Dad's protests. "They can't do this for me," Dad said. "There must be somebody else who needs help worse than I do." But they did it—three thousand bales of hay in two days. Dad said it was the most beautiful hay he'd had in years.

And now our neighbor's expression of love (and our family's livelihood) lay in a smoldering heap of ash.

We can still remember the dejected look on Dad's face as he helplessly watched the barn go up in smoke. But while we knew Dad felt the pain and frustration, he never said anything. He just got back on his feet and set about the task of rebuilding his farm. Somehow, some way, Dad managed to climb out of the ashes and set his face toward rebuilding our future. Dad was a living example of perseverance, of hard work in the face of long odds. He never gave up, not even a few years later when the new roof on our long chicken house suddenly collapsed under the weight of a heavy snow.

Dad competed daily as a farmer against both nature and adversity. Hard winters, continual equipment breakdowns, and unstable prices continually tested his will and determination. But Dad knew the meaning of hard work and he knew how to handle hardship.

We learned from Dad's example. We learned as we watched him get up every morning and go back out to work, even when things would break down or didn't go well. He would just continue plugging away until he accomplished what he wanted to.

Competing with the Hostetler Boys

Whether it was intentional or not, Dad passed his competitive spirit to all four of his boys. We were always trying to outdo each other. Even now, we compete in everything from backyard basketball games to golf. I can still recall seeing Jeff's competitive side the time he had to sink a fifteen-foot putt to beat me on the final hole of our annual Fourth of July outing at Sliding Rock Golf Course in the hills of the Laurel Highlands. Of course, I did everything I could to distract him just before he left-handed his putter toward the ball and hole. He had read the green perfectly and, although he got lucky when the ball caromed around the lip of the cup before it fell, I couldn't help but appreciate the stroke of competitive drive in him. Although it was just a fun family outing, Jeff savored beating his older brother. And I wasn't about to hear the last of it.

The competition in sports started long before that, however. It has a long and distinguished history.

Sunday Afternoon Football

It was fun watching Jeff grow and develop as part of our survival course in the Hostetler school of competitive drive. Especially while playing football in the backyard, older boys versus the younger.

Football in the backyard with the Hoss brothers on Sunday afternoon was sandwiched between church and chores. Our field was the place where Sunday school lessons of love, humility, and mercy slammed hard against personal pride, power, and conquest; where Mennonite beliefs of pacifism, restraint, and peace did battle with aggression, conflict, and anger. Ecclesiastes might say it was a season for everything under the sun: a season of laughing and crying, tearing and mending, trash talking and silence, dancing and mourning. And it continued, Sunday after Sunday, round after round, toe to toe, until old man winter sounded the final bell.

Driven by an insatiable appetite for competition, Jeff and Todd would challenge Doug and me to a game of backyard football, season after season, just for the opportunity to beat us. Jeff and Todd didn't seem to mind playing against us, even though we were bigger. In fact, most of the time they loved it. Even though Doug and I would play on our knees to make things fair, we never seemed to stay there, particularly if Todd or Jeff happened to break open down the sideline on a long run.

These weren't just touch football games, either. Doug and I really enjoyed hammering our younger brothers with forearms and body blocks. Yet they kept coming back for more, even though we occasionally slammed them into the electric fence that separated our yard from the cow pasture. Today I can see how this made Jeff tough—something he would need to play quarterback in the NFL.

Because we were bigger and older, Doug and I always got the best of Jeff and Todd. But I remember the day and the play when Jeff's competitiveness finally went into hyperdrive. As the old sports cliche goes, he was about to "make a statement." I had been knocking Jeff around pretty good one fine Sunday, until he finally got so angry that he decided it was time to make a stand. He took the ball and faked a hand-off to Todd, then kept the ball and ran straight at me. I waited for him to fake and cut away from me like he always did, but this time it didn't happen. With a look of determination and revenge in his eyes, he threw himself, kamikaze-style, hard into my gut, almost knocking me off my feet. Surprised and a little shaken, I countered with a forearm to his chest and watched him recoil in pain as he crashed to the ground. But he never cried or said a word. He just looked up at me with a look in his eye I had never seen before.

When he stood up I noticed for the first time how much bigger he had gotten. He wasn't my little brother anymore. He was almost my height, his legs were thicker and stronger, and his shoulders had broadened. So had his head and heart—both now seemed more determined and stubborn than ever, because he repeated the whole thing again. Once more, he ran right smack into me, hoping to catch me off guard and knock me down. But I recovered fast enough to put him on the ground once more, only this time it was a little harder than the last.

When Jeff stood up, he gave me that look again. It was a silent stare straight into my eyes that seemed to say, "C'mon, Ron. Give me your best shot—I'm ready for it. I can take it again and again until you can't give it anymore."

Thinking I had finally knocked some sense into him, I expected him to try something different the next play, like run to the outside. But he didn't. Incredibly, he ran straight at me again. This time, as he charged into me like a raging bull, I delivered a forearm into his chest with everything I had, expecting to flip him backwards. But it didn't happen. Instead, he dropped the ball, grabbed hold of me and tried to wrestle me to the ground. It turned into a minibrawl with us exchanging words as well as shoves and a few punches. When things finally settled down, the look in Jeff's eyes told me all I needed to know. From now on, things were going to be different. And they were. He was determined, and from that point on nothing would stop him.

Yes, Jeff Hostetler came by his competitiveness honestly. What he didn't inherit from Dad, he learned from his three brothers. And that prepared him for an outstanding high school sports career.

High School Competition

A graduate of Jeff's alma mater once observed, "As a ten-year-old, Jeff would often be seen throwing a football on the sideline behind the Conemaugh Township High School bench during his older brothers' football games. Sometimes he would throw as furiously as a relief pitcher in a bullpen. At other times, he would mimic his older brother Ron, who was the team's star quarterback. If Ron threw deep, Jeff threw deep. If Ron rolled right, Jeff rolled right. Sure, he was too little yet, but he wanted to play so much. Someday his turn would come."

How right she was. As surely as Jeff's day of standing up to me in our backyard football games would come, so would come the time when he would no longer mimic his older brother's moves in high school football. The day came when he would step out and establish himself as a high school sports star in his own right.

Jeff was an outstanding high school athlete from the very beginning, making the varsity football and baseball teams his freshman year in high school. (He had also done well in basketball, but freshmen weren't eligible for the varsity. And he also competed in track and field.)

In football, Jeff's competitive fires were whipped up during his freshman year when his coach moved him from quarterback to linebacker. Jeff was an outstanding quarterback—in junior high he had once made a seventy-yard touchdown play—but he would have to wait his turn to play that position in high school. And although he became a high school *Parade* magazine All-American as a linebacker, his life's ambition was to be a winning quarterback.

Basketball was easier for Jeff because he had no position problems. The only thing Coach Joe Majers wanted him to do was score and rebound. When he was a junior and Todd was a sophomore, they won the Jaycee Holiday Tournament basketball championship by beating North Star 78-41 in the final. Jeff was named the Most Valuable Player in the tournament, scoring twenty-seven points in the championship game.

During Jeff's senior year the Conemaugh Township High School basketball team went 23-0 for its first-ever undefeated regular season. The team then went all the way to the Pennsylvania Interscholastic Class AA finals at Civic Arena in Pittsburgh, where it lost to St. Pius X of Pottstown 57-52. It wasn't one of Jeff's better games—he missed a breakaway dunk during the game.

The loss still hurts Jeff and he was especially stung by critics who thought his attempted dunk was showboating. He wasn't showboating at all, but thought a dunk would give his team a lift. He later told a reporter, "I'd have done it again. It could have given us just enough momentum."

Jeff was also a standout in high school baseball, earning all-state honors as an infielder. In fact, he was so good that he got a letter from a scout for the Pittsburgh Pirates who asked him to consider a career as a professional baseball player. "I personally feel that you have the tools for a career in the major leagues," the scout said. "The opportunity will be there when you graduate to choose between football and baseball."

Jeff was an accomplished athlete on both the basketball court and on the baseball diamond and he loved both of those sports and cherishes the time he spent playing them. But his first love, his real passion, was football. When Jeff was little, he dreamed of playing high school football. When his chance finally came, he made the most of it.

Jeff wore number 3 in high school football, a symbol to him of being the third Hostetler brother to play quarterback and linebacker for the Conemaugh Township Indians. He was one of the best ever at Conemaugh. During his last three seasons there, he rarely came off the field, playing both sides of the ball in almost every game. For good measure, he handled the kickoff and punting duties as well.

The same competitive fire that marks Jeff Hostetler the NFL quarterback burned inside him on the high school field. One of the starkest examples of this: One Friday night during Jeff's sophomore season, the Indians played Windber, their archrival. With Conemaugh down 7-0, Jeff threw a touchdown pass to coach Joe Badaczewski's son, Mark, with just two minutes to go, making the score 7-6. Instead of going for a tie by kicking the extra point, "Bada" went for the lead with a two-point attempt. But the Conemaugh ball carrier was stopped dead in his tracks at the line of scrimmage and the Indians lost. The loss was hard on Jeff, but in his mind, going for the two-pointer was the right call—the *only* call. Jeff had taken the field to win, not tie. And he would rather have gone down trying to win than settling for a tie.

Conemaugh Township finished Jeff's junior year with an 8-1 record. Again, Jeff made the All-County team at quarterback…but there were changes coming for Jeff and his high school football career.

Despite Jeff's desire to play quarterback, Coach Badaczewski moved him to running back for his senior season. In hindsight, it was a good move for Conemaugh. Opponents, realizing Jeff was the team's go-to guy, put every player on him and used every defensive gimmick they could think of to pressure him. They would stuff the line with almost every player, knowing that Conemaugh couldn't win if Jeff didn't have time to pass.

Todd had been the team's backup quarterback and was Jeff's best receiver from his tight end position. But this year Todd would be asked to throw, not catch. Jeff really didn't want to make the move, but being the team player he is, he switched—although inside he knew it could hurt his chances of being seen as a prime college quarterback prospect, something he had established as a goal.

The move worked well for coach "Bada" and the team. Todd and Jeff became a wrecking ball of sorts for the opposition. As the season progressed, Jeff's rushing stats mounted, as did Todd's throwing marks. At the end of the season, the Southern Alleghenies Football Coaches Association voted Jeff the Most Valuable Offensive Player of the Year. He was also named to *Parade* magazine's High School All-America Team as a linebacker. Although those were great honors for Jeff, he still considered himself a quarterback, and he felt that he was just as good as the quarterbacks who made the *Parade* All-America Team: Dan Marino and John Elway.

At the end of Jeff's senior season, coach Bada said he thought Jeff could start on almost any major college team in his freshman year in a variety of positions. That was nice to hear, but there was only one spot Jeff had in his sights: quarterback.

A Legacy of Success

Jeff's competitive drive has produced a legacy of success at all levels of competition in football. That success has been achieved through perseverance, goal-setting, hard work, confidence in his own abilities, and faith in God.

While Jeff grew up in a family that refined and cultivated his competitive nature, he still had to decide what he would do with that part of his personality. Jeff chose to work hard at everything he did—from schoolwork to athletics—and the results speak for themselves. Even when things didn't go his way during his football career, Jeff chose to persevere and continue to work hard until good things happened to him. He chose to compete!

All of us have that same choice to make. Our Creator has lovingly allowed us to decide for ourselves how we will respond when things don't go the way we want them to. That doesn't just apply in athletics, either. It applies to whatever line of work you choose or whatever ministry you take part in. It applies to everything you do. Your choice is simple: You can take the easy road and give up when you encounter tough times, or you can decide to glorify God in what you are doing, dig in, keep working hard, and wait for good things to happen.

Jeff has had to choose many times how to respond when things weren't going the way he wanted them to. He could've said, "I can't," and quit when he took the poundings in our backyard football games. But he didn't. He hung in there and eventually he was able to compete with his older brothers. He could have said "I won't" when his coach asked him to switch from quarterback to running back. But he didn't. Instead, he complied with what the coach felt was best for the team and became the best running back he could be.

In these instances, Jeff chose to say, "I can! I will!" Such is the iron will that characterizes Jeff Hostetler, the competitor. This is what drives him towards excellence. And it's also the thing that helped him get through one of the toughest challenges a college quarterback can face.

CHAPTER FOUR

BEHIND COKE-BOTTLE GLASSES:
THE COLLEGE YEARS

I t was 1:30 P.M. on February 21, 1979, when Jeff Hostetler delivered himself and his football career into the hands of Joe Paterno and Penn State University.

The legendary coach had made a special trip through heavy snow to our farmhouse in Hollsopple to personally witness and bless Jeff's signing of the grant-in-aid that the coach and university were extending. It was a happy moment for our entire family and for our high school football and basketball coaches, Joe Badaczewski and Joe Majers, who were also present.

Jeff had done it. He had signed to play football at Penn State University, where he hoped he could follow in the steps of former All-American Lion quarterbacks Richie Lucas and John Hufnagle.

Penn State: A Family Tradition

It didn't surprise too many people that Jeff decided to play football at Penn State. The Hostetlers were a Penn State family. Doug and I had gone there on football scholarships and I think it was taken for granted that Jeff would follow in our footsteps. While he had been recruited heavily by Division I colleges across the nation—he made recruiting trips to Pittsburgh, Stanford, and Notre Dame—many schools backed off recruiting him because it was assumed that Penn State had the inside track. But that wasn't necessarily true. Like any high school athlete who is going on to compete at the collegiate level, Jeff had a decision to make, and having two brothers play at

University Park, Pennsylvania, wasn't a guarantee that Jeff would become a Nittany Lion.

It took Jeff much thought, prayer, and counsel from family and friends before he made his decision. He even received some advice from people he didn't know. An enthusiastic Penn State alumnus sent him a letter that gave him some advice on his decision:

> Let it lie in the hands of the Lord (Proverbs 3:5, 6). Don't let anyone persuade you into anything. Don't go to Penn State just because you're supposed to, on account of your brothers. Whichever school you choose to go to, go because the Lord and Jeff Hostetler want you to go there.

We were a Penn State family, as I said, but all of Jeff's family and friends wanted him to make the right choice for himself. We all wanted him to go where God wanted him to be. We also cared about the character and integrity of the coach and his program. Doug and I had based our decisions to attend Penn State partly on our admiration for the kind of man Paterno is and the things he stands for—especially his focus on academic success for his players, something that was important to our family. That same concern was important to Jeff.

But Jeff also wanted to go to a program where he had an opportunity to play quarterback, something he had dreamed of doing since he was a little kid playing catch on the sidelines during his older brothers' high school football games. And although all of us were confident Jeff had the ability to become Penn State's next All-American quarterback, no one knew for sure what was going on behind those famous Coke-bottle glasses Joe Paterno wears.

Preparing for Controversy

Doug and I enjoyed playing football at Penn State and we were successful there. But Doug didn't seem to adjust as well when Paterno switched him from quarterback to linebacker, as my backup. Doug was terribly disappointed by the switch because, like Jeff, he wanted to play quarterback more than anything. But transferring to another school back then wasn't as acceptable as it later became, so he stayed and worked hard to make the best of his situation.

Jeff didn't want anything like this to happen to him, so he and Dad made sure Coach Paterno and the reporters understood Jeff's intentions. "Jeff only wanted to go to college as a quarterback, and Penn State is recruiting him as a quarterback," Dad said at Jeff's signing. "He has an understanding that they'll let him stay at that position as long as he wants to."

Paterno seemed to get the message, and although he never directly promised Jeff he would play quarterback—anybody who has been involved in sports knows that anything can happen—he told him the policy at Penn State was to allow the player to stay at the position he preferred in his first year. After that, it was up to the coaching staff to decide where he should play for the benefit of the team. Jeff accepted that when he signed, because all he wanted was an *opportunity* to prove himself at quarterback. That's all he asked, and all any coach could realistically promise. In his heart Jeff believed that Penn State would grant him that opportunity, along with the room, board, books, fees, and tuition that came with it.

With his signing with Penn State complete, Jeff was feeling pretty good about his situation. Here he was, ready to head off to college with an opportunity to play quarterback for one of the finest programs in the nation. That was an exciting development for anybody, and especially a small-town boy like Jeff.

But before the ink had dried on Jeff's signing, controversy was brewing. Two stories were published suggesting that Jeff had signed with Penn State as something other than a quarterback. *Sports Illustrated* ran an item in its "Scorecard" section that said, "Penn State has signed lots of big linemen, the nation's premier tight end, Mike McCloskey, a hot quarterback prospect in Todd Blackledge, and a future All-America linebacker, Jeff Hostetler."

Linebacker Jeff Hostetler? Although Jeff was big and strong enough (six feet three inches tall) to play the same defensive position in college that he did in high school, he had no intention of playing that position at Penn State.

He said it up front and he intended to stick with it: *He wanted to play quarter-back in college!* After all, that's what he had signed up to do. In the end, regardless of the stories and his own doubts about his coach's intentions for him, Jeff set off to Penn State University, eager to write his own story in Penn State's record books.

The Lions had a tough season in Jeff's freshman year, including a humiliating 19-14 loss to intrastate rival Pitt. Jeff saw limited action at quarterback as a freshman and was glad for it. Actually, that was encouraging to Jeff, because Paterno was well known for not playing freshmen. Over the years this man had said many times that freshmen shouldn't even be *allowed* to play.

After Jeff's freshman season, Paterno said that he was determined to start the following year with a new starting quarterback and backup. Jeff wanted to be that starter, but he knew he had to perform head and shoulders above everyone else in spring practice in order to get a shot at starting in the fall. He had an outstanding spring, turning more than a few heads. Some of the Penn State assistant coaches even told him so. In their minds, Jeff had clearly out-performed Blackledge—but Paterno surprised everyone by saying he wasn't going to make up his mind until after the summer. Jeff began to wonder what was going on in Paterno's mind.

But again, despite having doubts about his coach's intentions, Jeff spent the off-season working like a madman to get ready for the upcoming season. He spent literally hundreds of hours that summer lifting weights, running, throwing the football, and practicing passing plays and studying defenses. He was going to do everything he could to be ready for the challenge that lay ahead.

Starting at Quarterback...

By the time preseason started, Jeff had worked himself into excellent shape. He went into training camp still carrying the goal of starting at quarterback for the Nittany Lions. Again, he performed well in fall practice and this time Paterno was ready to make a decision: Jeff would be the Nittany Lions starting quarterback.

Jeff felt great about earning the starting spot, even though Paterno had him looking over his shoulder constantly. He started the first three games his sophomore year as the Lions beat Colgate and Texas A&M, but lost to a powerful Nebraska team.

There's an old saying in sports about winning as a team and losing as a team. That's exactly what happened against Nebraska; the whole team fell apart. Even though Penn State was never hopelessly behind, the Lions just couldn't get anything going against the Cornhuskers. And as so often happens in a situation like that, the coach made a quarterback change. Without telling Jeff why he was doing it, Paterno sent in Blackledge. That was the beginning of the end of Jeff's dream of starting at quarterback for Penn State University. Although he played in some games later that season—he pulled out some crucial wins and was even named Outstanding Offensive Player for his performance in a game against Temple—he never started again.

Discouraged but not ready to give up his dream, Jeff continued to work hard in practice and do everything the coaches asked him to do. Yet he never got a chance to win back his job. When Coach Paterno promised Jeff he would play in the Fiesta Bowl game at the end of the year but didn't play him one down, Jeff walked off the field a frustrated and demoralized quarterback, doubting if he would ever get another chance to prove himself to Coach Paterno. He knew then that he needed to make a change. He decided that he would leave Penn State University to find a program that wanted him as its quarterback.

A Change of Scenery

None of us could understand what was going through Coach Paterno's mind during Jeff's sophomore year, and neither could some of the Penn State assistant coaches. Jeff's quarterback coach even told him, "Jeff, I don't know what to say. The way things are going here, I guess it would be best for you to leave, like you want to. We don't know what's going on."

Jeff turned to his family for support and advice. Mom communicated with Jeff almost weekly with telephone calls and notes, but she and Dad had agreed to let Jeff make his own decision. It was their policy that when they turned their kids over to a coach, they weren't going to interfere—and this wasn't going to be an exception. They would allow the situation to run its course. Only after Jeff was ready to make a decision to leave did they meet him at State College to talk to Coach Paterno.

Jeff didn't want to leave Penn State without talking to Joe Paterno about it. Frustrated and more than a little angry, Jeff still wanted to leave on good terms and wasn't interested in making a stink. He wanted to make sure that Coach knew that there were no hard feelings. So he and Mom and Dad met with Coach to talk about Jeff's intentions to transfer out of Penn State and why he was doing it. Although Coach Paterno said he understood why Jeff wanted to leave, he argued that Penn State was still the best place for him and that the quarterback job was still open. But Jeff had already made his decision. It was time to go.

Jeff was deeply disappointed in the situation, but he didn't allow himself to become bitter toward Coach Paterno. After all, this was the nature of big-time college football and there were no guarantees. So Jeff decided then and there to let go, look up, and get better. He refused to dwell on the past.

Why didn't Coach Paterno do more to keep Jeff at Penn State? Perhaps he didn't really believe Jeff would leave. Maybe he thought our family ties would be enough to keep him a Nittany Lion. We don't know. But we do know Joe later said that letting Jeff go was "the hardest decision I've ever had to make."

If Coach Paterno thought it was the hardest decision he ever had to make, you know it was much harder for Jeff. Yet Jeff (and Mom and Dad) knew it was a decision that was best for him. If he was to realize his dream of playing quarterback at the Division I level, he would have to move on.

West Virginia Bound

With his decision to leave Penn State behind him, Jeff was faced with finding the right program to transfer to. Back home, Coach Joe Majers was trying to persuade Jeff to look seriously at Notre Dame. In the end, our brother Doug played a huge part in bringing Jeff to West Virginia.

During his days of foraging financial planning services in the hills of West Virginia, Doug became impressed with the football program of

Mountaineers' Coach Don Nehlen. Coach Nehlen had come from an assistant's job at the University of Michigan to take the team to a 9-3 record and a Peach Bowl victory in his second season at West Virginia. Doug told Jeff, "This is a place and a program and a coach you've got to look at."

Jeff took a good look at West Virginia and liked what he saw. The Mountaineers had a strong program, outstanding coaching, and cared about winning. It certainly looked promising.

Coach Nehlen had a dream of making his team a national contender in Division I football, even though he had to work twice as hard an any coach in the country to recruit players from traditional Penn State territories. His dream was Jeff's dream, and right from the start Nehlen told Jeff he would be given every opportunity to become his starting quarterback. Again, that was all Jeff asked for and all Coach Nehlen could promise.

It looked like an ideal situation for Jeff. Coach Nehlen even promised Jeff he could wear the number 15 jersey he so badly wanted (it had been Doug's number at Penn State and it was Jeff's way of fulfilling Doug's dream, as well as his own). So Jeff made his decision—he was going to be a Mountaineer!

Waiting for His Chance—Again

While Jeff would have loved to step right in and begin playing for the Mountaineers his first year at the university, NCAA rules for transfers required that Jeff sit out for one year.

So while he couldn't play in the games, Jeff prepared for the following season by working out with starter Oliver Luck, a fine quarterback who was later drafted by the Houston Oilers. Like he had prior to his sophomore season at Penn State, Jeff spent hundreds of hours working out, throwing the football, studying playbooks, watching game films, and practicing pass plays. He wanted to make sure that he was ready to play before he ever walked into his first practice the following season.

During Jeff's apprenticeship year, he lived off campus in a little rented house and worked hard on maintaining his 4.0 grade-point average. Even if he couldn't play football, he could work hard at school, something that seemed to come naturally for him. Jeff also had further motivation for working hard in school. It was called the "Eddie Award," which was given to the best athlete with the highest grades. It was something of a family tradition for us. Doug and I had received it our senior years in college, and eventually Jeff and Todd did, too.

Later on, Jeff found the field of finance fascinating and knew he wanted to make a career of it. After he graduated from West Virginia University, the option of a Rhodes Scholarship also was open to him.

While Jeff looked forward to playing football the following season, his year off from competition was a good one for him. Through the hard work he put in that year—in the classroom, in the weight room, and on the practice field—Jeff was able to prepare himself academically and athletically for what lay ahead.

The Realization of a Dream

With his NCAA-imposed year away from football drawing to a close, Jeff was finally closing in on his dream of starting at quarterback for a Division I college football team. And for those of us who knew Jeff, it wasn't surprising to see it happen.

Why was it no surprise? Because people who know Jeff know he is a man who is willing to put in the work it takes to be successful at whatever he is doing; he will persevere, even through his own self-doubts and discouragement. Eventually, Jeff lived out his dream as the starting quarterback for the West Virginia Mountaineers.

Jeff lived out his dream because he was willing to work hard and not give up, because he was able to keep alive his vision for himself. That's the lesson his story has for all of us. Although few people get the chance to play Division I football, we all have our own gifts and abilities. If we are willing to apply ourselves to using our talents to be the best we can be, we can live out our dreams, just as Jeff did.

Planning for Success

Almost every athlete (or spectator) can point to some "miracle" in a sporting contest. We have miracle catches, miracle shots, miracle finishes. Jeff

Hostetler has seen some miracles of his own on the football field.

One of the most memorable occurred in Norman, Oklahoma, where Jeff made his West Virginia football debut against the Oklahoma Sooners. Talk about a point spread! Everybody agreed it would take a miracle to beat this perennial top-ten powerhouse.

But Coach Nehlen told Jeff and his teammates that they had a chance to beat the Sooners as long as somebody threw a football on the field. His players believed him and better yet, they delivered, engineering a stunning win over the Sooners.

Leading 20-14 at halftime, Jeff remembers thinking as he entered the locker room, *This is too good to be true. I don't want to blow this game.* So he just cleared his head and concentrated on each play. He forgot about the score and did what he was supposed to do, play football. And when the clock ran out, Jeff found himself on the headlines of sports pages across the country, lauding his brilliant performance and his team's upset of the year.

With the temperature on Owen Field in excess of 100 degrees, Jeff enjoyed the kind of day every college quarterback dreams of as a kid. He completed seventeen of thirty-seven passes for 321 yards and four touchdowns. His performance earned him the *Sports Illustrated* Player of the Week honor. While he wished Penn State no ill will, Jeff couldn't help but wonder what another coach—the one behind the Coke-bottle glasses—thought of his game against the Sooners. In his mind, Jeff had proved himself. He had the right stuff to be a successful major college quarterback.

How was Jeff able to come up with an outstanding performance against one of the nation's best teams? In a real sense, he planned for it. "Awake and asleep, I had planned this victory in such meticulous detail that actually achieving it meant far more to me than if it was something I hadn't dared hope for," Jeff said later. "All my dreams of glory, of vindication, and of fulfillment had come true. I learned that day that a dream you have dreamed for so long can be a triumph far more powerful than something wonderful that happens unexpectedly."

In a way, Jeff was doing what God once told the prophet Habakkuk to do: "Write down the vision and make it plain so that a herald may run with it. For the revelation awaits an appointed time; it speaks of the end and will not prove false. Though it linger, wait for it; it will certainly come and will not delay" (Habakkuk 2:2–3).

Jeff's vision was real. And even though it seemed to linger forever, he wouldn't relinquish his dream. And because he hung on to his dream, it finally came true.

A Dream Continued

Jeff's appointed time, the vision he had recorded and inscribed on the tablet of his heart and had waited so patiently for, had come. After two years of waiting, he was finally living out his dream. And it continued as West Virginia finished the season ranked eighth nationally with a 9-2 record. One of the Mountaineers losses came at the hands of Pittsburgh and Dan Marino. And the other? Well, it had something to do with the big, dark glasses vendors were selling at West Virginia's Mountaineer Field.

Yes, Coach Paterno had arrived in town, along with some of Jeff's former teammates. But it wasn't going to be a happy reunion, at least in the eyes of the media. It was tagged the grudge match of the century: Jeff versus Joe and Hoss versus Blackledge.

With my little brother's team setting to face off against my alma mater, you might wonder who I was rooting for. Well, for me, blood is thicker than water and although I'll always cherish my years and good fortune at Penn State, forever grateful for the lessons I learned and bowl trips I made, I was backing Jeff 100 percent. I hoped he could prove to the Penn State people that he was an outstanding college quarterback.

Jeff couldn't wait for the challenge. He wanted to prove himself to his former coach and team. More than anything else, he wanted to play well to show everyone he could do the job. He wanted some redemption. But unfortunately, Jeff wasn't in top physical condition for the game. A turf toe injury he suffered in the previous game, against Virginia Tech, had slowed him down and hampered his mobility. On top of that, he had been showing signs of illness (mononucleosis). Coach Nehlen wanted him to sit out and rest, knowing that most players find it difficult, if not impossible, to even walk with turf toe. But Jeff was determined to play. And he played his heart out.

At the time, both teams were 5-1, with Penn State ranked second and West Virginia third in the eastern standings of the independent schools. But in the end West Virginia's 60,958 fans went home disappointed, while Jeff went to the locker room to face the reporters and apply some ice to his toe, knee, and pride.

Jeff had an outstanding game, completing nineteen of thirty-seven passes for 250 yards. He mostly outperformed Blackledge, but that didn't matter to Jeff, because his team couldn't stick the ball into the end zone. The 24-0 final score fell heavy on Jeff's heart.

While reporters dug around, looking for some kind of malice or bitterness on Jeff's part, they found only graciousness and class as he spoke of his former team. "The only thing I liked about the game," Jeff said later, "was that a couple of dozen Penn State players took the time to stop in and talk to me on the way out to their bus. I really appreciated that." And when a reporter suggested that Penn State had got in a few late hits on him, Jeff said, "Penn State is a class team, and class teams don't do late hits."

I was proud of Jeff for speaking well of Penn State like that, even in the midst of his disappointment. It was a good example of how to tame our tongues, as the Bible puts it in the book of James. Jeff did just that, and I also think that what he said about Penn State came from his heart. He really saw the Lions as a class program.

Coach Nehlen told reporters after the game, "Jeff shouldn't have played today, but he wanted to so badly. Now he needs to get better." Jeff appreciated Nehlen saying that, but he told the writers he didn't have any excuses. I was proud of his response. To me, it was the mark of a champion and a future Heisman Trophy candidate who would emerge the next fall following a postseason Gator Bowl battle with Bobby Bowden's Florida State Seminoles.

Finding the Love of His Life

After West Virginia's loss to Pittsburgh, Coach Nehlen was asked to draw comparisons between Jeff and Panther quarterback Dan Marino. Here's what he said: "You may know more about Marino, but I can tell you Jeff is a great individual. He's the kind of kid you'd like your daughter to bring home."

As it turned out, Nehlen's words were prophetic.

As the Mountaineers prepared to meet Florida State in the Gator Bowl at the end of Jeff's junior season, Jeff had his eye on something other than the game at hand. She was the brown-eyed beauty he had first noticed at a basketball game party he had attended with Mom and Dad on their first visit to the university. It was Coach Nehlen's daughter, Vicky, and she had attended the party with her boyfriend, who was later to become her fiancé. Jeff hadn't seen her around much since that party. Other people said she was really shy—so shy that she wouldn't even come to the dining room when her dad brought some of the players over to the house for dinner. That was OK with Jeff, because he was kind of shy himself. He was also engaged to a wonderful hometown girl who was still attending Penn State.

Coach Nehlen brought Vicky along to the Gator Bowl—a game the Mountaineers lost to Florida State—and that gave Jeff a chance to get to know her a little better. Before long, he found himself caught up with more than just her looks. He was attracted to the kind of person she was (and still is). Jeff's feelings for her began to grow. Soon, Vicky's mother and chaperone, Merry Ann, noticed the glances and body language taking place between Vicky and Jeff. And it continued once everyone got back to Morgantown.

On their real first date, Jeff took Vicky to a seafood restaurant in Masontown, a little village just outside Morgantown. He enjoyed teasing her about dating one of her dad's football players.

(When asked later by a reporter what he thought about his quarterback dating his daughter, Coach Nehlen said, "It has its advantages. At least I know where he is.")

A Heisman Hopeful

Coach Nehlen and his daughter weren't the only ones who were going to see a lot of Jeff in the months that followed. Mike Ballweg, West Virginia's sports publicity director, made sure of that during Jeff's senior year. Wanting to promote Jeff as a Heisman Trophy candidate, Mike sent out a recording about Jeff that would be played on local radio stations. It used the *Bonanza* theme song and he called it "Hoss and the Cartwrights." Jeff was also pictured in press releases wearing a pair of six-shooters. It was a wild and crazy move, but it was typical of the state of West Virginia, which had on its hands a legitimate contender for the award that goes to the nation's most heralded college football player.

Jeff had fun with Ballweg's promotional antics, but he also had a senior season to play. And what a season it was!

A Payback for Pitt

After clobbering Doug Flutie and his Boston College Eagles 27-17 in the season opener, Jeff and his teammates saddled up for a Saturday showdown with Pittsburgh at home. It was a big game against a team that the Mountaineers hadn't beaten since 1975. Jeff and his teammates were ready!

Before a nationally televised CBS audience and standing-room-only crowd, the Mountaineers and Panthers fought to the finish like a pack of gunslingers at the OK Corral. When the smoke had cleared and the dust had settled, West Virginia was standing tall with a 24-21 win. The win had come on the boot heels of some last-minute heroics by Hoss and the rest of the West Virginia offense.

Behind 21-17 with ten minutes to play and starting from their own ten-yard line, the Mountaineers went to work. Jeff looked into the West Virginia huddle and said confidently, "We've got ninety yards to go. Let's do it!"

The Mountaineers' fullback gained sixteen yards on a draw play, followed by a ten-yard gain from their tailback, and then another big gain by the fullback. A few plays later, Jeff kept the ball on a fake and rolled outside for a first down in Pitt territory. It was a huge play because it had been third and long and the offense needed a first down to keep the drive alive. I remember that play well and so do my brothers, because we were standing along the sideline near the first down marker where Jeff was headed. As he lunged for the extra yard that got the first down, he went down right in front of us.

What happened next was a moment none of us will ever forget. The three of us instantly bent down to physically lift Jeff to his feet. It was like the four of us were back home in the backyard at Hollsopple.

After the "thataways" and "let's gos" from the three of us, Jeff ran back into the huddle, feeling great. Like us, he could see it was an upset in the making. It took Hoss and his boys five more plays—including the one pass Jeff completed on the drive—to get the ball into the end zone. Jeff scored the touchdown for his team on a six-yard naked bootleg around the right end.

Mountaineer Stadium erupted into a deafening roar for its team, and chills ran up and down our spines as we focused our eyes on Jeff kneeling in the end zone to thank his Lord.

It was the first time West Virginia had beaten Pitt in almost a decade, and for everyone in the state—even the governor—it was like winning the Super Bowl.

Returning to Penn State

Hoss and his boys, along with a host of loyal Mountaineer fans, rounded up another victory the next week against Bruce Smith and his Virginia Tech Hoakies. It was a good win for West Virginia, but Jeff couldn't help but think about his return the following week to Penn State's Beaver Stadium and all the hype that was sure to come.

Because he had handled the previous year's loss with so much graciousness, Penn State fans and players didn't see it as a grudge match. Although the Nittany Lions got tired of hearing Jeff's *Bonanza* theme song being played all week long, they didn't brand him with any cheap shots, either verbally or physically. As Jeff said the previous year, "Class teams don't do cheap shots."

In the end, the Lions prevailed 41-23 despite a courageous effort by Jeff and his team. But Jeff's stature, both on and off the field, prevailed also. After the game, some of the Penn State players walked over to Jeff to compliment him and tell him he played a great game. Like the previous year, that meant a lot to Jeff and to the family. Although I was pulling for Jeff, I was glad to see Penn State, its fans, and its players still exhibiting the kind of class and respect expected of them, win or lose. I think it helped all of us reconcile what once might have seemed irreconcilable differences. Any hurt feelings that might have lingered since Jeff left Penn State had been healed. That day, I was proud to be Jeff's brother *and* to be a Penn State graduate.

The Mountaineers lost the following week to Miami before finishing the season with wins over Temple, Rutgers, and Kentucky in the Hall of Fame Bowl. Like the previous season, West Virginia had finished with a fine 9-3 record.

For Jeff, though, it was over. His five years of turning trial into triumph in college football had ended. Jeff finished his two-year career at West Virginia having passed for 4,055 yards and 24 touchdowns. For two years in a row, Jeff was an All-American. He finished fourth in the Heisman Trophy vote his senior season and played in two all-star games, the Hula and Japan bowls.

But this ending, like all others, was the beginning to something new. Jeff had some wonderful changes ahead.

Entering a New Line of Work

Like a trapeze artist floating high in the air above the crowd after letting go of one bar to catch another, Jeff was poised in midair. Between the letting go of his past and grabbing on to his future, there was no turning back. There *would* be transitions in Jeff's life.

Still, Jeff had been here before. He had learned something about transitions—partly with the help of the man in the dark, Coke-bottle glasses. He had learned that whether transitions in life led to ruin and despair or renewal and hope depended on attitude, vision, patience, hard work, and an iron will to get there.

That's part of life for all of us, really. Ready or not, changes and transitions are going to come. If we are armed with faith in God and the will to work through the rough spots and make changes when needed, we can get through the transitions successfully. Jeff did!

With college football behind him, Jeff had a vision of the future for himself—and he wanted to share that future with Vicky. So in May of 1984, at the Missionary Alliance Church in Morgantown, they initiated a marriage covenant in the presence of God and more than 300 people (including Senator Jay Rockefeller), promising to put their faith, fidelity, and love to work.

Marriage is a total commitment for Jeff and Vicky, a "till death do us part" promise that they never intend to break. Jeff and Vicky both realize that marriage, like any worthwhile endeavor, takes work, hard work. Jeff is one of those fortunate few who had a wonderful example of how to make a marriage successful and happy.

He couldn't have had a better model than Mom and Dad. Although sickness, financial setbacks, and the stresses and strains of farm life threatened to break apart Mom and Dad's marriage many times, they stuck together and worked through their difficulties. The glue that held them together was their covenant commitment, the promise they made to God and to their friends and family that they would do whatever it took to make their marriage work. No doubt they sometimes felt their relationship was more like marital bondage than marital bonding. But bailing out was never an option for them.

It's an option Jeff will never consider, either. That makes Vicky and the three boys feel secure. Mom always used to tell us that the best gift we Hostetler men could ever give our children is to love their mother. (Mom knew about these things.) And if there's one thing that is certain in Jeff's marriage, it's that he will love Vicky through everything, that he'll remain a devoted and compassionate husband—even in the toughest of times.

A Final Word

With his college football career over, Jeff had one last official function to perform as a Mountaineer before he moved on. He was selected to give the keynote speech at the National Football Foundation and Hall of Fame dinner at the Waldorf-Astoria Hotel in New York, honoring the country's top scholar athletes.

In his speech, Jeff told the sixteen hundred people in the grand ballroom what he believes with all his heart and practices with all his strength: "I believe God has given us the gift of life, and it is up to us to become the best that we can be. It is our choice to do what we want with our lives. What a man can be, he must be. No one else can do exactly what you can do. You are unique. Therefore, I dare you to become the best in the world at whatever you choose to do."

Those are such powerful words, especially coming from someone who dares to practice what he preaches. Jeff still challenges those around him—and those reading this book—to honor God in whatever they do, to be the best they can at what they are doing so that God can be glorified. That was his challenge to the men and women who listened to him speak that day in New York, and it remains his challenge today.

With that speech delivered, it was time to move on. It was time for Jeff to start his career in the National Football League.

CHAPTER FIVE

ONE GIANT LEAP:
ON TO THE NFL

While Jeff and Vicky honeymooned on the island of Saint Martin, owners, coaches, and player personnel of the NFL's twenty-eight professional football teams were busy at work lining up their picks for the 1984 college draft. On draft day each team's coaches and scouting combines put their homework and fieldwork on the line for all the world to see. For the teams it was a time of boom or bust, depending on what kind of players their picks turned out to be.

Much like Dad's old grain combine during harvest time, the scouts work to sift, thresh, and harvest stalks of talent. This demands a critical eye, attention to detail, a sound knowledge of the game of football, keen judgment, and sometimes a little luck. Teams look for impact players—all-around athletes with great speed, size, quickness, intelligence, strength, and work habits—who can provide an immediate lift.

For the professional football player, being a high pick is a lot like winning the lottery. It's a goal of all the top college players to be drafted in the early rounds, thus ensuring a big payday. So when scouts step on campus with their stopwatches and clipboards, every athlete does his best to impress them. Some players do crazy things to cast themselves in a better light. I remember some of my Penn State teammates hiding weights in their athletic supporters to add a few pounds when they were weighed. Others put one-inch strips of felt in the bottom of their socks to give them a boost in height.

Most scouts perform a battery of tests to evaluate a player's flexibility, agility, and leaping ability. Some even give personality tests to determine a player's desire, intelligence, and work and nutrition habits. Talk about an audit! By the time they are finished, players wonder if the scouts know them better than they know themselves.

Draft Day Disappointment

Like most highly-touted college seniors, Jeff had his sights on the NFL. As an All-American in both his junior and senior seasons, he was projected to be a high pick, unusual for a West Virginia player. Coach Nehlen used to talk about how scouts go to some programs such as Penn State and Pittsburgh to look at maybe seventeen kids, but that when they come to West Virginia, they have no expectations.

It's still that way. Penn State has consistently been listed in the top five of all collegiate programs in terms of numbers of players in the NFL. The list of former Nittany Lions in the NFL is long and distinguished: Franco Harris, Jack Ham, John Cappalletti, Curt Warner, and, most recently, Kerry Collins. Those are just a few of the former Penn State players who went on to star in the pros.

West Virginia, on the other hand, has turned out only a few NFL greats, Sam Huff and Daryl Talley being among the most notable. Oliver Luck, who preceded Jeff as the Mountaineers starting quarterback, also played briefly in the pros. Still, West Virginia is clearly not in Penn State's league when it comes to putting players in the NFL.

Jeff was hoping to be an exception to all of that. Yet he knew that although most scouting combines had projected him a first-round pick, and possibly the first quarterback to be drafted, anything could happen. The word on the street (and from his agent, Rob Bennett) was that the Giants were very interested in getting Jeff in the first round if he was still available. Jeff knew about the rumors and was optimistic they would become fact. Jeff was just hoping for a solid team and an opportunity to eventually start and win a Super Bowl ring.

When NFL Commissioner Pete Rozelle stood at the podium in the ballroom of the Omni Park Central Hotel in New York City on draft day of 1984 and announced that Michigan State linebacker Carl Banks was the Giants' first choice, Jeff's heart sank. His disappointment deepened as the first round came and went without his name being called. Jeff began to wonder what was going on and so did all of us sitting around the television set with him in Coach Nehlen's home in Morgantown.

Deeply disappointed and discouraged, Jeff had to get out of the house as the first round of the draft came to a close. He and Vicky went for a walk to talk about things.

All of us shared Jeff's disappointment. We believed he was good enough to be taken in the first round and we couldn't understand what was happening.

While the previous year's draft had been top-heavy with quarterbacks—Dan Marino and John Elway were two of the six quarterbacks drafted in the first round—the 1984 draft was defense oriented, with not a single quarterback taken in the first round. In fact, the first quarterback drafted that year was Maryland's Boomer Esiason, by the Cincinnati Bengals in the second round—the thirty-eighth pick overall.

Our disappointment deepened as the second round came and went without Jeff being called. Finally, after fifty-eight picks, the New York Giants selected Jeff with the third pick in the third round, their third pick overall. It was quite a disappointment to Jeff, who believed he would be picked much sooner.

Still, Jeff's agent worked out a deal with the Giants comparable to that of a first-round pick. Jeff received a $300,000 signing bonus and a salary of $125,000 for his first year. While still disappointed that he was picked so late in the draft, the contract was salve to Jeff's wounds, considering he had never seen so much money in his life. "In Hollsopple, you would have to work all of your life for $300,000," he said.

Off to Training Camp

With draft day and the contract signing behind him, Jeff now set his sights on his next goal: making the team for the New York Giants. Jeff had graduated into the tough and demanding business of professional football. It was one giant leap into a world that offered no guarantees, just an opportunity. But that's all Jeff wanted. Now he was going to get it.

Jeff knew the Giants already had a solid and capable quarterback in Phil Simms, who was entering his sixth season in the league. But while Simms was a quality quarterback, he also had a history of injuries, having missed most of the 1983 season, all of the 1982 campaign, and parts of the previous two years. Jeff certainly didn't wish for more injuries to Simms, but at the same time he knew that his opportunity to play for the Giants might come sooner than later if Simms went down again. From all appearances, Jeff was the Giants quarterback of the future. The Giants had said that Jeff was the best quarterback in the draft when they took him, and Jeff assumed he was heir apparent when Phil Simms' career came to a close.

But before Jeff could think about starting (or even playing) in an NFL game, he had to take a tough, yearlong course called "Being a Rookie." His orientation would consist of a bit of brutality called preseason training camp, held at Pace University in Pleasantville, New York. I don't care who you are, where you come from, or what position you play, your first training camp is tough. It's like boot camp. It's filled with a daily regimen that pushes players to the limit—mentally, physically, emotionally, and, yes, spiritually.

For Jeff, it wasn't so much the physical aspect of training camp that made him suffer most. That part was tough, but he had dealt with it before. For him, the struggle was the mental aspect of camp. When you're in an NFL training camp, you're away from your wife and family for a month and a half. You're with the same guys the whole time and you can never get away from them. You work together and live together, all the time fighting each other for jobs. Each man in camp knows that players are going to be cut, and that if it happens to you, it's going to mean the end of everything you've worked for through high school and college. That's a tough thing to think about when you try to go to sleep at night on a hard training camp bed.

A Bible verse kept Jeff going during these torturous days. Joshua 1:9 says, "Have I not commanded you? Be strong and courageous. Do not be terrified; do not be discouraged, for the LORD your God will be with you wherever you go."

The great thing about being a Christian when you're in the middle of something difficult is knowing that God is there, giving strength and comfort as you struggle through. Jeff learned that early in his life and it was something he held fast to during training camp.

Breaking Camp

After camp, the Giants and the rest of the NFL moved on to their yearly schedule of preseason games. These contests give the veterans a chance to "tune up" for the upcoming season while the rookies, many of whom are still fighting for jobs, get one last chance to show the coaches what they can do. Jeff never really had a chance to show the coaches anything, however; he wasn't playing at all. Nor did that change in the regular season, as Simms played every series but one that year. He set several club passing records, leaving Jeff Hostetler and fellow backup Jeff Rutledge glued to the bench.

It was hard on Jeff to not be playing. He was giving his best and doing everything the coaches asked of him, and more. He struggled with not knowing what Coach Parcells had in mind for him. He began to wonder if he had ended up in the right place. In fact, he began to have doubts about his own words when he would speak to groups in college as a Mountaineer Christian athlete at West Virginia. He would tell people that God had blessed each person with certain abilities, and whatever they were, it was up to us to use them to the fullest. He'd say God had a perfect plan for us and while we may not always know what it is or why it is, down the road it would become clear. We just have to have the patience and the determination to believe in the abilities the Lord has given us and not get down on ourselves or let others get down on us. If we never waver in our belief, it will all come out right, not only for ourselves but for others.

At this point in his life, however, it didn't seem like things were working out and they certainly weren't clear. Jeff believed his work mattered to God and that every worker should be valued, but he also felt insignificant, useless, and not valued. Circumstances beyond his control—his playing time—clouded his vision of God's purpose for him.

Although Jeff believed training was essential for growth and development, he began to question the good it would do if he never got a chance to prove himself. And although he believed that the purpose of life and a life of purpose can only be experienced through service to mankind, he had the feeling he wasn't contributing a lick.

This was the yardstick by which Jeff measured his work as well as the work of his employer, the New York Giants. He was there to make a contribution to his team and community, provide for his family, and serve the God who made him, for as long as they wanted him there. But it didn't seem to him that they wanted him very much. His giant leap from collegiate to professional football appeared to have taken two steps backward.

Jeff was learning a hard lesson that all of us must master. Everybody loves mountaintop experiences, but no one lives on the summit; some of life must also be lived in the valley. In Jeff's case, graduating from West Virginia was a mountaintop experience; that's why he believed the words he had spoken to others in college. But mountain tops don't last forever, and upon Jeff's entrance to the valley of struggle in the NFL, his faith was tested once more before the next mountaintop arrived.

When you're going through a difficult test like that, however, it's hard to think in such positive terms. All Jeff could see at the time was that his career seemed to be unraveling fast. He didn't know it, but he was about to enter a time of testing that made his struggle in the NFL look easy. He and Vicky were about to take a frightening detour on their journey as parents.

From the Mountaintop to the Valley Floor

I remember Jeff's phone call the night of June 11, 1985, when he awoke me with the good news. He and Vicky had just delivered a son, Jason. Man, was he excited! His voice was filled with energy and exuberance as he told me about his experience. I loved hearing him talk about what it felt like to be a dad.

Jason's birth was like a ray of sunshine for Jeff and it seemed for the moment to dispel the dark shadows lurking in his football career. After Jeff and I finished talking, I went to sleep thanking God for the precious gift he and Vicky would enjoy in the coming years.

But in the morning Jeff called again and there was something different in his voice, something that told me instantly that something was terribly wrong. Jason had been diagnosed with some serious heart problems and he might not survive. Jeff asked me if we would pray for his son.

Again, Jeff had gone from a mountaintop to a valley floor. But this time it wasn't something as temporal as a football career. This was his son! His own flesh and blood was fighting for his life and nobody knew which way that fight would go.

Back at Valley Hospital in Ridgewood, New Jersey, the doctors worked frantically to find the problem as Jeff and Vicky huddled together in disbelief. It just didn't seem real. Before they even had a chance to hold Jason, he was whisked away to intensive care. Now, their first baby—the little boy they had waited so long to hold—lay in an incubator, IVs sticking out of his little arms. He looked a deathly blue. Worst of all, they weren't allowed to pick him up or hold him.

Jeff felt crushed as he looked at his newborn son with all the tubes and wires sticking out of him. Jeff felt empty, helpless, and in disbelief as he prepared himself and his wife for the battle ahead.

Jason was later transferred to Columbia Presbyterian Children's Hospital in Manhattan. Jeff took Vicky home to her family; she couldn't handle staying in a hospital ward full of healthy babies and exuberant parents. Who could blame her?

After caring for Vicky, Jeff left for the hospital. He was hoping for some answers…and a miracle.

The surgeon told Jeff that Jason had pulmonary stenosis, a narrowing or closing of the pulmonary valve that leads from the right ventricle of the heart to the lungs. The surgeon explained that the valve was dangerously narrow and that very little blood was getting through it, so Jason wasn't getting blood oxygenated through his lungs. This was the reason for the blue tinge on Jason's lips, skin, and nails.

The surgeons performed surgery to try to open the passageway on Jason's tiny heart, but that was far from the end of the struggle for Jason. Two weeks after Jason's first surgery, he had to endure another operation, this time a small bypass.

Jason was fighting a courageous battle and so was Jeff. He visited the hospital every day for two weeks, asking questions, requesting consultations, and encouraging a son who would get to know his daddy's voice: "Hang in there, buddy," Jeff would whisper. "You're going to do fine." But even Jeff had trouble believing those words. *Would things be fine? Would we get to take Jason home?* he wondered. Jeff's faith was going through a test like never before.

Although the second operation went well, Jason lost a kidney when a blood clot lodged in an artery leading to the organ. It had formed at the end of a catheter used to monitor his oxygen levels and had dropped when the doctors removed the catheter.

By now, Jeff and Vicky just wanted to get their son home. Finally they got their wish. But five months later, Jason was back in the hospital, this time with a blockage in his bile ducts. He was terribly jaundiced and doctors said they needed to find the blockage and remove Jason's gallbladder. On the day of the surgery, Jason's blockage passed but the doctors removed his gall-bladder anyway to prevent a reoccurrence of the problem.

Jeff and Vicky suffered incredible anguish during and after Jason's series of painful surgeries. They could tell how painful it was for their little boy and they shared in that pain. But they also shared with one another the feeling that they weren't doing enough, that there was something more they could do to ease their little boy's pain. Their baby wasn't even six months old but he had already lived through more pain than most people see in a lifetime.

For the next several months Jeff and Vicky and the doctors monitored Jason's progress. Back home in Morgantown, Jason's size and strength seemed to be growing, just like Jeff and Vicky's optimism. But when a heart catheterization performed to check how his heart was doing revealed more trouble, Jeff and Vicky found themselves taking one more step backward.

They set out to find the best surgeon in the country to do the procedure. They found him right in their own backyard at West Virginia University. A man in Boston who was supposed to be the authority on this kind of surgery recommended the surgeon, saying, "You'll be in the best possible hands with him." It was good advice.

Although the procedure to correct Jason's pulmonary valve and right ventricle went well, it was a long operation and hard on Jason. Jeff and Vicky still have pictures of Jason before the surgery, snapshots showing a plump, healthy baby boy. Pictures of him taken after the operation show a radically different story. Jason seemed to have become smaller and yet older. He'd lost a lot of weight and he showed plainly he'd endured a long year. Yet he pulled through it and that was the last of the operations.

He had made it!

Enduring the Pain

The ordeal took its toll on Jeff and Vicky. All of us felt like helpless strangers looking in from the outside. As much as we tried, we couldn't really know what they were going through.

Pain can be a terribly lonely thing, and I remember not having much to say when Holly and I visited Jeff and Vicky in New Jersey while they were struggling to make sense of things. Jeff doesn't say much to begin with, so it's sometimes hard to know what he's thinking or feeling or how to respond. I remember asking how I could help as we barbecued chicken on his grill from the deck out back. He told me that our presence was reassuring. When I asked how all of this was affecting his relationship with God, he answered me honestly, telling me that Jason's ordeal had been a test of his faith, one that he could very well have failed. Then he turned away, looked up toward the sky and said, "I wanted to turn my back on God for allowing this to happen. But when I did, it was worse. There was complete darkness."

Even Mom—the one person we could always count on to see something positive in the worst of situations—was at a loss to explain what God had in mind through this situation. She was a bedrock of support for Jeff and Vicky, sending them Bible verses and inspirational writings. But even she acknowledged being confused, puzzled, and even angry at God.

Mom had so many questions and despaired almost to the breaking point. But through it all, she held fast to her faith, believing that something wonderful would come out of such a dark time for Jeff and Vicky. She knew pain personally and if anyone could understand how Jeff and Vicky felt, it was her. Jeff remembers her telling him, "The Lord has a perfect little plan for Jason, even though we don't know exactly what that is. We should rest in that plan."

Jeff found that hard to understand, but it was all he and Vicky had to hold on to. Jeff had momentarily looked away from God, but what he saw was far worse than the ordeal they were going through. It was complete, utter darkness. There was no hope, no light at the end of the tunnel, no comfort in their time of suffering. Without their loving heavenly Father there to walk them through the wilderness, they had only the bleak prospect of muddling through alone.

Mom and Dad later gave Jeff a birthday gift he will always cherish and turn to in times of crisis. It was a book titled, *When There Is No Miracle: Finding Hope in Pain and Suffering*, by Robert L. Wise. Along with the gift she penned her thoughts: "To our dearly beloved son and his precious wife, as they've gone through so much pain in the last ten months. A normal person would have collapsed, but you two have the inner strength needed to survive. We praise our loving God for you and our grandson Jason." After describing her personal battle with faith, she penned her summation: "But always My Lord has helped me. I know He's holding you too. I know already lives have been changed because of your intense suffering."

Jason has since recovered completely. Although the trauma inhibited some of his early growth, he's healthy and active and plays soccer, basketball, and baseball. He also memorizes Scripture like a scholar. To Jeff and Vicky, Jason is a real miracle child.

Gratitude to a Faithful God

Jeff and Vicky have a hard time putting into words how grateful they are to God for healing their little boy. They're also grateful to the Lord for bringing them through the ordeal of not knowing if Jason would survive, of seeing him suffer, and of wondering if they could carry on in their faith.

As they look back on their experience with Jason, Jeff and Vicky have learned some very vital things about themselves and about their Lord. The most important lesson they learned, though, was that God is faithful. Even when they wanted to look away from Him, their heavenly Father was faithful. He didn't get angry with them when they doubted; He simply showed them that He loved them and Jason more than they could comprehend, and that He was their only hope for getting through the test that was the start of Jason's life.

That really put Jeff's struggles in his early NFL career into perspective. It was as if God were saying, "Jeff, someday you just might have success in your chosen profession. But I want you to know that no matter what happens in your career, it won't mean anything unless I give it meaning. Without Me, your career is nothing more than time passing."

This perspective said something about Jason's suffering, about Jeff and Vicky's suffering, and about how God can give it meaning. It said that all suffering can be something more than just sorrow and pain if God is part of it.

When Jeff wanted to turn his back on his heavenly Father, he saw something worse than his son's scars. He saw his own. He saw both a lost and hurting world scarred with hurt, anger, pain, and confusion. Worse than that, he saw this world had no hope! But he also saw his and Jason's only hope: the nail-scarred hands of another Son, the Son of God. Only through Him could they find any hope, meaning, or significance in Jason's illness.

Look beneath Jason's scar now and you'll find more than a heart of courage; you'll find the fingerprints of the Divine Surgeon who had worked secretly and quietly behind the scenes to work a miracle. You'd find those same fingerprints on the heart of a young man who didn't quit when his NFL career went into cardiac arrest. That's what gives Jason's ordeal and healing and Jeff's struggle and victory meaning.

This is the perspective Jeff has carried with him since winning the Super Bowl, and it is this perspective that reminds him of his worth, purpose, and aim. Perhaps it's said best by writer Annie Dillard, whose words Mom copied in her personal journal: "If, however, you want to look at the stars, you will find that darkness is required."

CHAPTER SIX

BACKING IT UP:
SUPER BOWL AND BEYOND

I t's been said that what doesn't kill you makes you stronger. Jeff and Vicky not only survived their ordeal with Jason, they grew stronger in their relationship with their Lord because of it. That strength was a blessing over the next several years, as Jeff and Vicky continued their journey of seemingly taking two steps backward for every one step forward in Jeff's career with the Giants. Every step was a test of faith.

Back to the Grind

With Jason's struggles now a memory, Jeff entered his second season with the Giants in the hope of earning the team's number two quarterback spot.

As it turned out, Jeff's position with the team didn't change that season. In fact, he wasn't even taking any snaps in practice. The only time he got to throw the ball was while warming up and during an occasional individual drill. For a quarterback, that spells disaster, since the only way to improve is through repetition.

When Jeff saw he wasn't going to play at quarterback, he made it clear he was willing to move to another position, just to get in the games. He volunteered to play on special teams or play receiver. The Giants put him on the punt-return team and when a couple of receivers got hurt, he volunteered to run the plays. Since he has great hands and knew all the routes (quarterbacks need to know these things), Jeff performed well and got to play in several games.

At last, he was playing *somewhere!* Making a contribution to the team helped relieve some of the frustration Jeff felt at not playing at his natural position. It felt good for him to be contributing in some way.

The Giants eventually made the playoffs as a wild card team, but lost to the Chicago Bears to end their season. As he packed his things for home, Jeff hoped for a real shot at the Number Two job the next season.

During the off-season, Jeff worked out hard as he always did. He determined to get in top physical condition, he worked on his game, and he kept plugging away to improve his chances of success.

But upon his return to camp the following season, Jeff felt like Bill Murray in the movie *Groundhog Day*. History repeated itself all over again. The only thing that changed was Jeff's health—he broke his leg when he was hit going across the middle to catch a pass in a game at San Francisco. It was the thirteenth game he had played as a special teams player and receiver that year. The injury ended his season and put him on the sidelines for the Giants' run through the playoffs and their 39-20 win over the Denver Broncos in Super Bowl XXI. All Jeff could do was watch and wait for the next season.

Next year, Jeff thought. *Next year will be different.* It had to be. It marked Jeff's fourth year as a New York Giant and in Jeff's mind it was a "do-or-die" season. Four years in the NFL is usually considered enough time for a quarterback to develop into a starter. A quarterback who spends more than four years on the bench is thought of as a long-term backup and not a potential starter. Jeff didn't want any part of that.

New Season, New Hope

Jeff had an excellent preseason camp and when the smoke cleared he had earned the number two quarterback spot. At last Jeff's career was moving in the right direction! But it wouldn't last.

Late in the 1988 season, Jeff got a rare chance to play against the New Orleans Saints when Simms was injured. Jeff had a respectable first half, completing five of his ten passes for 128 yards, including an eighty-five-yard touchdown to wideout Stephen Baker. With the first half over, Jeff headed to the locker room feeling pretty good about his performance.

But as Jeff walked through the tunnel toward the playing field to begin the second half, Coach Parcells walked up to him and said he was going to put in third-string quarterback Jeff Rutledge. Jeff was in a state of shock. He couldn't believe what was happening, and, apparently, neither could his teammates. About a dozen of them walked over to Jeff to find out why he had been taken out of the game.

Although the Giants eventually came back from a 9-7 halftime deficit to win the game, Jeff was too upset to enjoy it. He was not only sick inside, but angry. He appreciated his teammates' support, but that didn't relieve his frustration. What did he have to do to prove himself worthy of his coach's confidence? Would he ever enjoy a successful career in the National Football League?

Jeff was so frustrated and angry that he called his agent and asked that Giants General Manager George Young trade him. When Young said no to a trade, Jeff decided to stick it out for the rest of the year, hoping for a trade in the off-season. Without free agency in place, Jeff couldn't just walk off and sign with another team. If he left the Giants, he would have to leave football for good. And since he wanted so badly to play, he decided to stay.

For their part, the Giants showed no desire to get rid of Jeff. After the season was over, they decided not only to keep Jeff on the roster but to protect him from being claimed by other teams before the next season. Jeff interpreted the move as a good one. To him, it meant the Giants valued his services and potential.

Jeff proved them right during the 1989 season, stepping in to win a couple of games when Simms got hurt again. He finished the season having completed twenty of twenty-nine passes for a quarterback rating of 80.6. (A quarterback rating takes into account statistics such as completion percentage, touchdown passes and interceptions, yardage, and so on. Joe Montana was the top-rated quarterback in the NFC that season with a rating of 112.4. Simms' rating was 77.4.) It lifted Jeff's confidence, as well as that of the players and coaches, that he could play well when given a chance. It gave Jeff added encouragement that he contributed to a team that finished 12-4 and won the National Football Conference Eastern Division.

But that was just the beginning. Bigger and better things were to come in 1990. That was the year Jeff finally escaped his sideline prison.

Getting His Shot

Ten games into the 1990 season, the Giants found themselves celebrating a 10-0 record and entertaining visions of another Super Bowl berth. Three games later, led by the passing of Phil Simms and a tenacious defense anchored by All-Pro linebacker Lawrence Taylor, the Giants were riding high with an 11-2 record and heading into a fateful game at Giants Stadium.

None of the Giants had any idea that their starting quarterback would go down for the season with a severe ankle injury when the Buffalo Bills came calling on December 15. At the time, it seemed like a terrible blow for the Giants. It was the fourteenth game of the season and there was no way Simms could be ready for the playoffs.

But Jeff was ready. His years of hard work and preparation for this very moment were about to pay off big-time. Jeff stepped in to finish the game and although the Giants lost to the Bills that day, it would be the last time any team—including the Bills—would get the best of the Giants that season.

History records how Jeff went on to help lead the Giants to regular season-ending wins over the Phoenix Cardinals and New England Patriots to finish 13-3. They then took NFC playoff victories over the Chicago Bears and San Francisco 49ers to earn a spot in Super Bowl XXV.

Perspective from an NFC Championship

The 1990 NFC championship game was a memorable one for Jeff—and for me. It was a classic matchup featuring a last-minute Giants drive for Matt Bahr's game-winning field goal to send New York on to the Super Bowl. But out of that game came not just memories of a great contest. It also was a time where God used something as insignificant (in the eternal context) as a football game to show Jeff something about what he was to learn from what had happened in his career and to his son.

John Madden wanted to interview Jeff after the game, so I waited for Jeff with my son Jared. We played catch with the football—the same ball that Bahr had kicked through the uprights to win the game—while we were waiting. I threw a perfect strike down the sideline to Jared, who caught it, ran into the end zone and spiked it. I laughed, then glanced to the lower seats in the bleachers to see if Madden and Jeff had finished their interview. Then I looked into the stands and lights. By now it was dark, but you couldn't see the stars because of the lights. Everyone had gone but a few custodians sweeping up. I closed my eyes for a second or two and took it all in.

Beating Joe Montana and the 49ers had been an amazing feat for Jeff and his teammates. Nobody thought it would happen, but it did.

Jeff missed the team bus because of his interview, but Madden drove him to the airport in his cruiser just in time to catch the flight out of San Francisco. Moments later, as we banked high above Candlestick Park on our flight, an amazing thought hit me, a thought that started to put everything into perspective: *Things look different up here. Candlestick Park doesn't appear as big and the lights aren't as bright as they were on the field after the game.*

Lengthening shadows now cradled the stadium, like a mother putting her child to bed. It had been a tiring but eventful day. As much as I wanted to kick back and sleep, I couldn't. The shadows of Candlestick wanted to tell me something. So I listened. And what I observed while they tucked away a piece of sports history right before my eyes was extraordinary.

You see, to millions of people that NFC championship game was the manifestation of an idea, a picture of what professional sports should look like. In essence, it represented the epitome of what the game *should* be: Two teams with high-powered offenses, great defenses, and brilliant coaching, battling for supremacy. The game featured spectacular plays, last-second heroics, and a Cinderella finish for the Giants. In the eyes of Giants fans, it was a monumental event, one more step that moved them closer to the grandaddy of them all, the Super Bowl. But for 49ers fans, it was a heart-breaking loss.

Those shadows blanketing Candlestick Park made me wonder: In an age where "image is everything," was there anything substantive about this game in the eternal sense? Or was it form without substance, a mere passing shadow?

My answer came within moments. As our plane leveled off at 30,000 feet, I was no longer looking down upon the shadows of Candlestick, but out at an endless expanse of universe. Peering into the starry blackness, I heard a still, small voice say, "All of life is but a shadow—form without substance—unless the shadow reflects this eternal reality: Behind God there is nothing else."

As much value as we put on the things in this life—family, friends, career, sports—without God, it all adds up to nothing. And as great a game as that NFC championship was, it adds up to zero unless God gives it value. As well as the athletes may have played in that game, their performances meant nothing unless God gives them meaning. And as great as the glow may have appeared on the faces of the victors, the victory is empty unless the face of God glows within their hearts and homes.

You Did a Good Job

You've already read how Jeff led his team to the NFL championship in Super Bowl XXV. It was obviously the high point of his NFL career so far. Jeff was wined and dine and celebrated for weeks because of his performance. But not everyone joined in on the festivities.

Coach Bill Parcells has never been one to dish out much praise to his players. He didn't speak to Jeff at all after Super Bowl XXV until the next morning when he saw him in the hotel. "You did a good job," he said. That was it.

Coach Parcells' most ardent words of encouragement to Jeff came after the Giants win over Phoenix in Jeff's first start that season. He told Jeff how much he had appreciated his attitude over the years. He went on to compliment Jeff on how he prepared hard, worked hard, and when the opportunity came, he took advantage of it. He finished by saying, "You've proved to everybody that you can play in this league."

With two wins in the playoffs and a victory in the Super Bowl, Jeff had indeed proved that he could play in the National Football League. It was a great accomplishment for the Giants and Jeff had a big hand in it, completing twenty of thirty-two passes for 222 yards and a touchdown in the biggest game in all of professional football. Jeff Hostetler had done what only the most fervent optimist believed was possible. His run through the playoffs that season will live as one of the great stories of all time in the National Football League.

But as the Giants players and coaches headed their separate ways following their second Super Bowl win in five years, there remained a nagging question: Would Jeff Hostetler remain as their starting quarterback when the 1991 season kicked off that fall?

A New Era in New York

Although the press hyped a quarterback controversy during the off-season, Jeff dismissed it, knowing he probably wouldn't be the starter the following season (at least not at first). Jeff realized a couple of things about the way things worked in the NFL. First, Parcells had his loyalties, and one of them was to Phil Simms. Second, it was considered more or less standard operating procedure that when a player lost his position due to an injury, he is given a chance to earn back his job. Phil Simms was still a proven quarterback who once earned the MVP award in the Super Bowl.

Jeff was aware of all of these things and he gave them a lot of thought in the weeks after the Super Bowl. Still, he realized they all fit under the heading of "Things I Can't Control." All he could do was spend the off-season preparing the best he could, work as hard as he could in preseason training camp, and let things develop.

But when Parcells resigned at the end of the season and General Manager George Young hired Ray Handley to take his place, Jeff figured he might get a shot as the starter. He was right, as Handley announced that Jeff would be his starting quarterback.

When Handley made his announcement, Jeff was elated but others were shocked. Handley noted how Jeff had proved himself in the playoffs and pointed out that Simms was 36 and had lost a lot of his mobility. No, Jeff would be the Giants quarterback—not of the future, as he had been for the previous seven seasons, but of the present. It was the beginning of a new era for the Giants, and for Jeff.

Winning and Losing

Winning a Super Bowl was the highlight of Jeff's athletic life. It culminated years of hard work, sweat, and testing. But in some ways, winning a Super

Bowl can almost be as much of a curse as it is a blessing. Winning a Super Bowl means that you've set high standards for yourself and nothing short of winning "the Big One" will be enough to satisfy.

Jeff learned about that in the following two years.

Jeff played well for the Giants during the two seasons following the Super Bowl. Of New York's fourteen victories during those two years, twelve came with Jeff as the starting quarterback. In 1991 Jeff started twelve games for the Giants and set a single-season club record for completion percentage, 62.8, on 179 of 285 pass attempts for 2,032 yards and five touchdowns. He also set a Giants single-game completion percentage record of 82.3 with a 28-of-34, 368-yard performance against Dallas. His interception percentage of 1.4 was the lowest in the NFL that year.

His next season, Jeff played in thirteen league games with nine starts for the Giants, completing 103 of 192 passes for 1,225 yards and eight touchdowns—a 53.6 completion average. He threw only three interceptions, equaling the Giants record for all-time low in that category, and his 1.6 interception percentage was the best in the entire NFL among passers with over 175 attempts. He was the Giants third-leading rusher that season with 172 yards on 34 carries for a 5.1 average, scoring three touchdowns.

But there was a downside. Jeff missed several games due to injuries, the worst of which occurred in Tampa Bay, where he suffered a back injury that required him to be taken off the field on a stretcher. Later, the MRI (Magnetic Imaging Resonance) test revealed several finger-like cracks along some of Jeff's vertebrae in his lower back. The injury wasn't career threatening, but it put Jeff on the sidelines for the rest of the season.

Meanwhile, the once proud Giants struggled, going from Super Bowl champions in 1990 to 8-8 also-rans in 1991. It got worse in 1992, as the Giants finished 6-10.

And as the Giants' fortunes declined, the criticism increased.

New York can be a great place to play professional football, but it can be a tough place, too. That's because the fans and the media expect the best and they aren't going to put up long with losing. Winning truly is what counts in the National Football League and when you're winning, few are going to say anything critical about you. But when you're losing, the criticism can be brutal.

Jeff had to listen to a lot of criticism during the Giants' two seasons after the Super Bowl. It got so bad that disgruntled fans would drive by Jeff's home and curse at him and call him names while his sons were playing outside. The abuse got so bad at the games that Vicky stopped taking the boys.

In New York, it's not only unruly fans you have to deal with. The Big Apple also has the biggest, nosiest, and noisiest press in the country. With so many newspapers, magazines, and radio and television stations, professional athletes are constantly under a microscope. Worst of all, writers are so competitive for big stories that some will stretch the truth or simply write stories with no basis in fact. Because they appear in print, however, people take them for gospel and believe every bit of them.

Jeff had to live through all the criticism and doubts from the fans and the media. He understood that was part of the business, just like being treated as a hero was part of winning the Super Bowl. He didn't enjoy being criticized, but he took it like a man and didn't let anybody see that it was really hurting him inside. It's called growing thick skin.

While Jeff had his supporters in the New York media, not making it to the Super Bowl was dividing everyone into three camps: Jeff Hostetler supporters; Phil Simms supporters; and Ray Handley haters, who began chanting "Ray must go! Ray must go!" at the games.

According to the press, someone had to go. Ray did, and so did Jeff…but on his own terms. Feeling that it was time for a change, for the Giants and for himself, Jeff shopped his services around in the free agent market.

Free at Last

The word *freedom* means different things to people. To a player in the National Football League it means one thing: The opportunity to shop your services around a league in an open, fair, and competitive marketplace. It means finding out what you are worth and who wants you. Different teams in the league had expressed interest in Jeff, and with the Giants hedging on their interest in him, he felt it was time to shop around. For Jeff, entering the free agent market in 1993 was a lot like the college recruiting he had gone through during his senior year in high school.

When Jeff signed with the Giants, he hadn't figured on leaving. But he realized that the NFL is, after all, a business, even for a proud organization like the New York Giants. Jeff had planned on making a career of it in New York, mostly because when he signed, free agency had not yet been adopted in the NFL. At that time, a player was in total subjection to the team that held his contract. He either played where they wanted him to play, for however much money they decided to pay him, or he didn't play at all. A player's only other option was to play in the Canadian Football League.

But with the implementation of free agency, Jeff became a free agent and was in good position to test the free agent waters. He jumped in the pool.

An Interview with the Raiders

As he shopped his services around among several interested teams, Jeff was invited to Los Angeles for a "look see" by Raiders President and General Partner Al Davis. Al was looking for a quarterback who could help fix his broken-down team, an able-minded, able-bodied leader with the kind of initiative and know-how to put some air back in a franchise that had gone flat. What he discovered on Jeff's trip, figuratively speaking, was a humble farm boy who knew how to do just that.

After picking Jeff up at the airport, Al's limousine blew a tire on the expressway. To make matters worse, the limo driver didn't know how to change it. So instead of waiting around while the cars and time blew by, Jeff decided to do something. He got out of the car, rolled up his sleeves, and went about changing the flat like an Indianapolis 500 pit crew mechanic, while passing motorists flew by within inches of hitting him.

This is the kind of work ethic that Jeff learned on the farm. When we were kids, the farm machinery needed repair from time to time, often in the middle of harvest. We didn't have time to wait for professional mechanics to come fix the machines, so we became "do-it-yourselfers" out of necessity. That's still the kind of person Jeff is today. When something needs doing, he does it.

Al Davis needed this kind of ballplayer, someone who didn't give excuses, someone who could get it done now, someone with a work ethic and the motivation to get it done when it needed to be done. Davis believed he had found that kind of player after his first meeting with Jeff; Jeff thought the same about Al Davis. Sure, there were the stories about Al's methods and meddlings in operating the Raiders and there was criticism of Bay Area fans when the club moved to Los Angeles from Oakland. But one thing was sure: Al wanted to win, and so did Jeff. From all appearances, Al valued his work and his workers, walked his talk, pursued loyalty and excellence, believed in the value of training, rewarded good performance, and worked to serve the needs of his team. Jeff shared the same ideals, the same guiding principles.

The principles and character qualities that helped Jeff Hostetler win a Super Bowl in New York were the same ones that so impressed Al Davis when the two men met. Jeff was about to embark on another chapter in his life—both as a child of God and as a professional football player.

It was time to head west. Jeff was going to be wearing the silver and black of the Los Angeles Raiders (soon to be Oakland Raiders once more).

CHAPTER SEVEN

BILLY SUNDAY:
SHARING CHRIST ON THE FIELD

Name-calling scorches your ears. Fists fly. Nasty hits and gang-tackling break out everywhere. And that's just in the stands!

Welcome to Oakland Alameda County Coliseum, Jeff Hostetler's Sunday house of worship.

This particular day wasn't your typical church service. It looked more like a rock concert, with its wild-eyed, shirtless, body-painted, body-pierced, boisterous, barbaric fans moshing it up and jumping around. And yes, they can rock the house.

But on this day they were there to watch their Raiders rock the San Diego Chargers 17-7 in the 1995 regular season opener and to celebrate the team's return from Los Angeles to Oakland—the first game at the Coliseum in fourteen years.

Lifted emotionally by a raucous crowd that arrived early, cheered their warmups, and then provided high-decibel support at every crucial moment of the game, the Raiders did everything they needed to do—including marching down the field for a beautiful ninety-nine-yard touchdown drive—to defeat the defending AFC champions. Jeff played a solid game for the Raiders, completing fourteen of twenty-six passes for 136 yards.

The ninety-nine-yard drive was huge for Oakland. Pinned at their own one yard line, the Raiders at least had to move the ball far enough downfield to give their defense a shot at stopping the Chargers. As Jeff later put it, that was a huge "attitude" drive for Oakland.

Having the Right Attitude

Ask any National Football League player what is required to be successful and one thing likely to be near the top of the list is attitude. It takes a certain frame of mind to successfully play a tough, violent game called professional football.

Players do all kinds of things, some of them downright bizarre, to get themselves in the right frame of mind to play a game. Some players resort to self-inflicted mind games to get themselves ready. Others engage in superstitious pregame rituals. Still others allow the crowd, be it friendly or hostile, to get them ready. All of this in the name of attitude.

What drives Jeff's attitude in this setting isn't the raucous crowd nor any mind game or superstition. Jeff gets himself in the attitude to play football by remembering Who's watching from the Sky Box. And I don't mean team owner Al Davis, but the real Owner and Creator of everything, the One Who watches from His permanent Sky Box in heaven. In Jeff's mind, He is the One who called and gifted him for his work on the football field. And in many ways it's like the work of an evangelist.

Hitting the Sawdust Trail

Jeff realizes he's playing football to lead his team to victory, but he also wants to lead people to the Son of God. In many ways, Jeff is like Billy Sunday and his sawdust trail.

Who is Billy Sunday, you ask?

He was a professional baseball player-turned-evangelist who lived from 1862-1935. He played for the Chicago White Sox, the Philadelphia Athletics, and the Pittsburgh Pirates during his career.

Billy Sunday lived a remarkable and tough life; that was part of what made him the man he was. At the age of ten, he was placed in an orphanage because his father had died from pneumonia while serving in the Union Army and his mother was unable to provide for their large family. While there, he learned to work hard with his hands.

Billy became a success in professional baseball through hard work and determination, as well as amazing foot speed (he could circle the bases in just fourteen seconds). Like so many of the players of his day, Billy Sunday not only played hard, he partied hard. That all changed after Jesus Christ became his Lord and Savior. Jesus didn't just save Billy; He gave him a call to the full-time ministry. One day Billy bid professional baseball and the saloons good-bye and hit the "sawdust trail" as an evangelist.

"Hitting the sawdust trail" was the phrase used to describe people who got up at an evangelistic meeting and started down the aisle to commit their lives to the Lord. The phrase originally came out of the Oregon forests, where lumberjacks who would get lost deep in the forest would find their way out by following a trail of sawdust. The phrase took on a whole new meaning for Billy Sunday. Most of the "tabernacles" Billy preached in had sawdust on the floors to cut down on the dust and to cushion the sound, and when people got up and started down the aisle, somebody said they were hitting the sawdust trail. The phrase stuck.

While Billy Sunday left the life of professional baseball, he still used his considerable athletic ability in delivering his messages. He acted out stories and Bible vignettes, giving them breathtaking vigor as he skipped, ran, walked, bounced, slid, and gyrated all over the platform. He would pound the pulpit with his fists, impersonate a sinner trying to reach heaven like a ballplayer sliding for home, and illustrate his points by running and sliding the length of the stage. Every story was an athletic pantomime performance. He certainly kept people awake!

During his time as an evangelist, Billy Sunday spoke to an estimated one million people, an impressive number when you consider he lived in an age without microphones, television, radio, or public address systems. It was just one human being trying to contact other human beings in order to help them find their way back home to the Lord.

Today, there's another Billy who enjoys making contact with other human beings in large meeting places on autumn Sunday afternoons. He's also a hard-working boy who labored hard with his hands and who runs fast (at least he used to) and uses his athletic skills to keep the gathered crowd awake and bring glory to God—he's *William* Jeffrey Hostetler, the National Football League quarterback.

Going into All the World, One Sunday at a Time

As a child of God, Jeff knows he is called to obey Jesus' command in Mark 16:15 to "Go into all the world and preach the good news to all creation." Those are heavy words indeed, and words that all of us who call Jesus Christ "Lord and Savior" are to obey.

Why is it that so many of us don't even try to preach the gospel? Do we think we're too busy or have too many family commitments? Are we convinced we just don't have time to lay aside specifically for preaching the good news of salvation?

In my book those are pretty lame excuses, and here's why: Jesus calls us to preach the Word and glorify Him in *everything we do!* We are to let our words and our actions proclaim the truth that Jesus has made a way to the Father in heaven by His death and resurrection, and we are to do it in whatever we do and wherever we are. We are to preach the gospel in the office, at home, at school, at the gymnasium—everywhere!

Jeff understands that, and he knows that God has given him special abilities and opportunities to bring glory to Him in what he is doing right now, playing professional football. He may not be an evangelist in the same sense that Billy Sunday was, but he knows that he still has the opportunity to let his words and his actions proclaim the gospel of Christ.

Don't misunderstand; Jeff's first priority when he's on the football field is to do his very best to help his team win. That's part of his job description and what he's paid to do. It's sort of like that with his home life too. Jeff's priority as a husband and a father is to do the very best he can to have a winning family life. That's the commitment Jeff made to Vicky before God and his friends.

Jeff has these different priorities in his life, but there's a bigger picture here. He knows that as he gives everything he has to be the best he can be in these areas, he is at the same time bringing glory to God. Colossians 3:23 tells us that we are to work hard at whatever we do so that we can glorify our Lord. And that is exactly what Jeff does (and what we all should do) in whatever he does.

Some people might argue that Billy Sunday's work as an evangelist was more important that Jeff's work as a football player. The problem with that kind of thinking is that it assumes the only way we can communicate the gospel of Jesus Christ is to go into "full-time" ministry. Yet we are called to preach the gospel of Christ *wherever* we are and in *whatever* we are doing. For that reason, Jeff's work (as well as our own) is just as important and valuable to God as that of a pastor, teacher, or evangelist. The same is true of an auto mechanic's, a garbage collector's, or a housewife's work. If that's the work God has given us and we are performing it to win—doing the best we can where we are and with what we have, to the glory of God—then it's important work.

Working for Spiritual Growth

Jeff realizes that it takes hard work to keep him growing and keep him from sinning. The life of a professional athlete is full of temptations. The money and fame can become a curse if they are not managed properly. Sadly, many professional athletes, even Christian men, have fallen because they either didn't realize this or because they knew it but didn't heed it.

Jeff understood these things when he came into the league. Early in life he learned the principles that have kept him from giving in to temptation. So, if you don't mind, let's go back again to life on the farm to see how God instilled into Jeff's heart the principle of working hard on the spiritual part of life.

Knowing God on the Farm

We learned much about spiritual discipline as we were growing up. We learned at a very early age that God was going to be a big part of our lives. As a Mennonite family, this was demonstrated big-time on Sunday mornings at the Hostetler home.

On Sunday the family was closest. It was the day we could sleep in until 8–8:30 instead of getting up at 6 A.M. like every other day. There was no grading of eggs on Sunday morning. Mom and Dad always got up first and while Dad went out to feed the chickens, Mom put on some music and began to fix breakfast. When Dad came back in, he began to make his rounds to wake up his kids. He made a big thing of it. The first time he came to our rooms, he told us to wake up. The second time, he turned on the lights. The third time, he grabbed the covers off the bed. The fourth time, you got up.

Then we all got together at the table for Sunday morning breakfast. Meal times—breakfast, lunch, and supper—around the old cherry dining table at the Hostetler home were always special. For us, meals were oocasions for fun and fellowship, for spending quality time with one another. Mom always made sure everybody was at the table before we started eating. To her, this was our special time for togetherness.

After breakfast it was time to get ready for church—and you can be sure missing church wasn't an option. We never missed church, at least not that we can remember. On Sunday mornings, we were always at church, at least in body. Even though we weren't allowed to miss church, we usually found ways to miss the sermon. The messages often got too long and boring (for the kids, anyway), so to pass the time we would sleep, play tic-tac-toe, make paper airplanes, and shoot spitballs with our friends in the back row. In summer, when things really got hot and boring, we would look for and occasionally catch a big horsefly to have some fun with. We would pull some thread from our socks or shirt, tie it around the poor thing's leg, and then let it go. The sight of this often reminded us of the airplanes that flew up and down the Atlantic coast beaches, with their banners trailing in the wind. It sure got people's attention. Now and then one of our flies would wing its way toward the pulpit, distracting the crowd and pestering the pastor.

We meant no harm in doing these things at church. We were just bored and wanted to go home. We never wanted to go too far when we were cutting up in church, however, because if Mom or Dad caught us—and that happened on occasion—they would get up from their seats, walk back to us, grab us by the ear and walk us up to sit with them. Now that was embarrassing!

Over the years we sat up enough and listened enough to the sermons that some of what was said sunk in. One evening, during a service in our public high school, Jeff heard and responded to a message that changed his life, completely and forever. It was the night he made a public confession of faith in Christ Jesus as Lord and Savior.

Jeff had always been a sensitive and quiet kid growing up. But after he committed his life to Christ, he became more sensitive to spiritual things. He acquired an appetite for reading God's Word, for prayer, and for going to church. He also became more keenly aware of sin and its impact. To this day, none of those things have changed.

Making his personal commitment to Jesus Christ changed Jeff's life forever. And as he continued to grow physically, he also grew spiritually.

Growing in the Faith—In College

When Jeff left home for college, he took his faith in Jesus Christ with him. He continued to grow in his faith as a member of West Virginia University's chapter of the Fellowship of Christian Athletes.

As a star athlete on the West Virginia football team, Jeff was a popular speaker in churches and meetings around the area. He and two of his teammates—Paul "Woody" Woodside and Dave Johnson—would hit the road as a speaking team on as many nights as they could manage. This trio always had a great time on their speaking trips. Johnson, West Virginia's center, was Jeff's roommate, and each of them owned a Fiat. Despite their cars' frequent breakdowns and ailments, they could usually count on one of them to and from where they were going to speak. Mostly, they spoke to church groups and youth organizations in the Morgantown area. Their only payment was a nice lunch or dinner before they had to start back home.

Of course, the people of West Virginia loved their football and their players and wanted to hear all about Mountaineer football. They always listened closely to Jeff, Paul, and Dave, hoping to hear something about football.

When Jeff spoke, he tried to remember the things he learned at home from Mom and put them into his own words. He remembers speaking about one of Mom's favorite passages in the Bible, the thirteenth chapter of 1 Corinthians, which talks about the importance of faith, hope, and love, and how love is the greatest of them. He would remind his audience that the most precious things in life are the people you love: husband, wife, children, parents, good friends. He would remind people that the ones we love are precious gifts from God and that they should never be taken for granted.

He's still making that point today. Jeff says, "I believe God has blessed each of us with certain abilities, and whatever your ability is, it is up to you to use it to the fullest. God has a perfect plan for you, and right now you may not know what that plan is or why God has it, but down the road it becomes clear. We must have the patience and the determination to believe in the abilities the Lord has given us and not get down on ourselves or let others get down on us. We have to feel we are worthwhile. If we do, if we never waver in our belief; it will all come out right not only for ourselves but for others."

Jeff will always remember his trips with his two friends as rewarding times, not because they received any financial compensation, but because they felt that they were giving something back to God and to the people of West Virginia for all that had been given to them. The speaking engagements were also a wonderful time of growth for the three men. Most memorable to Jeff is how Paul overcame a stuttering problem that was so bad that it was almost impossible to understand him. After going with Jeff and Dave on those speaking trips for a year or so, he began speaking as though he never stuttered.

His college years provided special times of growth and fellowship for Jeff and his Christian brothers. When he moved on to the National Football League, he continued in his faith and fellowship.

Room for Jesus in the NFL

As a quarterback in the NFL, Jeff has seen and felt some incredible violence perpetrated by some of the biggest, strongest, fastest, meanest men in the world. Obviously, pro football isn't a profession for the faint of heart.

But in addition to that, Jeff has also enjoyed some of the greatest experiences of his life with men who share his faith in Jesus Christ. He has seen for himself that some of these incredible hulks are also sensitive, loving men of God who, like Jeff, want to do everything they can to win those around them to the Lord.

Even after winning a Super Bowl, Jeff still says one of the most memorable things he has seen in his days in the NFL is a baptismal service some of the Raiders held in the team's locker room Jacuzzi. About twenty players took part in the service. Jeff remembers how the power and love of Jesus was expressed in so many remarkable ways. Men gave testimonies of what Jesus meant to them and others rededicated themselves and their work to the Lord.

Like the rest of the world, though, the NFL can be a tough place for a Christian to live out his faith. In addition to the temptations that come as a result of the money and fame, the schedule for a professional football player can hinder him from doing the things he would like to do as a man of God and as a husband and father.

Life in the NFL can present a problem for Christians in that their schedule keeps many of them from attending Sunday church with their families. Being a dedicated family man and believer, Jeff doesn't like that he must miss church with his family during football season. But he understands, as do his wife and children, that playing on Sunday is part of the deal of being a pro football player.

Jeff fills part of the void left by missing Sunday services through attending his team's pregame chapel services with about twenty of his teammates. They usually gather for about an hour on Saturday evenings, after the Raiders' team meeting, to pray and worship together. They usually bring in a guest speaker to give a message.

These guys are serious about their faith and their families. Knowing the precarious nature of their work, they seek whatever strands of faith, hope, love, and encouragement to keep them going (and performing well) that they can find. They find it in the chapel services.

Learning Accountability

For the Raiders, Steve Wisniewski, a Penn State graduate, usually leads the chapel services and lines up the speakers. He's been like a brother to Jeff in addition to being a good Christian friend. He's a great example of something that Jeff holds as very important in his life: accountability.

To Jeff, "Wizzer" embodies everything that can be said about loyalty and accountability. On the field, he is the enforcer, Jeff's personal bodyguard. Steve is a good Christian man with a heart for the Lord, but he can become like a grizzly bear on a bad hair day when it comes to protecting his quarterback. Once when an opposing player hit Jeff out of bounds, Steve—all 300 pounds of him—was ready to exact retribution. Like a shot out of a cannon, number 76 was right there, making sure that the defensive player who made the late hit understood why he wouldn't be doing it again. When Jeff saw the play the next day watching film in the locker room, he just smiled. Here was a friend who would shed his blood, even give his life, for him.

And Steve keeps Jeff accountable.

Accountability is very important to Jeff, as it should be to all of us. Accountability means you have someone to answer to, someone you'll allow to challenge you in your faith and in your walk with Christ. That is the kind of relationship Jeff has with Steve Wisniewski.

Accountability and the Blood Drill

When I think of accountability, I think of a little Penn State football tradition called "Blood Tuesday."

"Blood Tuesday" was the day our linebacking corps did some smash-mouth, face-busting, toe-to-toe hitting and tackling. It was a day for high-octane collisions as we propelled ourselves into one another, kamikaze style. Does it sound violent? It should. But it wasn't mindless football brutality with no purpose. It was a day for getting better, for sharpening our skills and our appetite for perfection. That's what the coaches wanted and demanded on Blood Tuesday: Perfection. No mistakes. No defects. Just flawless, unsurpassed excellence.

Our linebacker coach, Jerry Sandusky, conducted a drill on these particular Tuesdays to bring out that kind of perfection. Appropriately enough, it was called "Blood Drill."

"Blood Drill" was a three-on-one contest. In this drill, Coach Sandusky would stand behind the single player and direct the other three facing him to attack on command. That single linebacker, standing one step from the others, would have to "read" each attacker's approach in an instant, step up, deliver a counter strike, and then gather and realign himself as quickly as possible to meet the next attacker. It was a rapid-fire drill that tested strength, leverage, quickness, balance, agility, perception, ability to adjust, and especially toughness.

"Blood Drill" was also something of a rite of passage for Penn State linebackers. It required using the forehead of the helmet with such force and in such a way that it would often tear the flesh right above the bridge of the nose if you performed it correctly. When you felt the hot blood drip down your face, you knew you had become a blood brother, a lifetime card-carrying member of the Penn State linebacking corps.

I remember my first "Blood Drill." When I was done, I certainly didn't want to do it again. I suffered a slight concussion, whiplash, and cuts and bruises on my arms. It wasn't until about a year later that Jerry danced around me, yelling and hollering because I had done the drill right. And I guess I had—I was bleeding from the bridge of my nose.

While the Blood Drill was a painful, sometimes ugly part of practice at Penn State, it was effective. The idea was to keep drilling and trying until you perfected your linebacking technique. It wasn't an easy drill, to be sure. Sometimes you'd get knocked down or even knocked out of practice. But if you didn't quit, you could master the drill. The idea behind Blood Drill was simple: Excellence requires repetition—and someone or something to challenge you, sharpen your skills, and toughen you up. "Blood Drill" provided both.

In a very real sense, we all need something like that in our Christian walk. We all need someone to run the "Blood Drill" in our lives, someone who will hold us accountable, challenge us, toughen us up—and even rough us up when we need it.

Proverbs 27:17 says, "As iron sharpens iron, so one man sharpens another." This means that we all need someone who will look us in the eye and challenge our thoughts, intentions, motives, and behavior; someone who will ask the tough questions, challenge our choices, and help decipher our decisions. We need someone who cares enough to demonstrate "tough love" when it's needed.

Jeff and I have been blessed in this area. Mom and Dad demonstrated this kind of love. So did our brothers and sisters. Our coaches did, too. They challenged us, reprimanded us, and encouraged us to get better and to perfect our attitudes, skills, and behavior.

We didn't always like it. At times we thought they were cruel, unkind, and uncaring. But these people could sense when we needed to be challenged and when we needed an encouraging word, when we needed discipline and when we needed a pat on the back, when we needed practice and when we needed rest, when we needed to be pushed and when we needed support.

As a full-grown man with a family, Jeff is no longer accountable to his parents, brothers and sisters, or high school coaches, at least not the way he was as a boy growing up. That is why having Christian friends who will hold him accountable is so important to Jeff. It helps keep him answerable to someone who cares.

Staying Behind the Scenes

On one of the walls of Jeff's home back in Morgantown, West Virginia, hangs a lithograph portraying a father kneeling in prayer at the bedside of his sleeping child. In the background is the image of an angel of light raising a hand against an angel of darkness, preventing the evil spirit from penetrating the child's world.

This image is a serious reminder (given to Jeff by Mom and Dad one Christmas) of the spiritual battle we are all in. It also reminds him of the necessity and power of prayer as he lives out his football life before the eyes of the world.

God is watching Jeff from His sky box. So are a cloud of witnesses that surround him on any given Sunday during the season. Jeff is doing his best to run his race with endurance, all the time fixing his eyes on Jesus, the author and finisher of his faith.

Sometimes my little brother "Wilbur" (one of our nicknames for him) gets tired of the cameras and media hounds capturing his every move. There's not a lot of privacy for the professional these days. But for now, he's making the most of the time and platform he's been given as he travels from one meeting place to the next, Sunday after Sunday. And even in between.

For example, in 1996 Jeff wanted to do something special at Christmas for some underprivileged and financially needy children, so he took them for a shopping spree. They were allowed to get any gift they wanted. It broke Jeff's heart to see a little girl pick up a beautiful, expensive doll and put it back down because she thought it cost too much. With a smile on her face and tears in her eyes, her Mom assured her it was OK to have the doll if she really wanted it. That picture will live forever in Jeff's heart. But there was another part of this story: Jeff wanted to make sure that the children understood the true meaning of Christmas, so he bought each of them an illustrated children's Bible and signed it for them.

These are things that often go on behind the scenes and Jeff wants to keep it that way. It's why he founded the "Hoss Foundation," a nonprofit ministry to help people wishing to adopt children and to meet the financial needs of children with handicaps.

I'm proud to watch Jeff, not just on the football field, but as he uses the gifts God has given him to preach the gospel. I'm also challenged by his example. Jeff has been a demonstration of something we all need to keep in mind: That in whatever we do, wherever we are, we can obey Jesus' words to "preach the gospel."

So next time you see Jeff raise his hands on the gridiron and point his fingers to the sky in thanks, jubilation, and praise, remember that he's just honoring his Father, remembering why he's here, and trying to direct his chorus of followers heavenward—down the sawdust trail to a place where they can find their way back home to the Lord.

CHAPTER EIGHT

KEEPING YOUR FOCUS:
WHEN LIFE PLAYS ITS PRANKS

J eff got the word. He was to report to the front office.

This usually meant trouble, big trouble. And he had a hunch he knew what it was about.

No, this wasn't the office of the Oakland Raiders. Jeff wouldn't be seeing the inside of that room for many years. This was the principal's office at Conemaugh Township High School. The principal had just learned about Jeff's escapade in the hallway—of dousing a fellow student with a mouthful of water that he had so expertly fountain-headed through his front teeth.

The shot could've won awards. It carried from Jeff's position in the hall all the way into the classroom. And the kid who got it had asked for it. Catching Jeff's eye as my brother walked by on his way to the restroom, the student made an unseemly gesture at him from his position in the classroom. The principal didn't care much for the incident, or for Jeff's side of the story. All he knew was that he couldn't have Jeff (or anybody else, for that matter) creating a disruption like that.

Jeff soon found himself on the principal's black list. Before long, he was being called into the principal's office for things he wasn't doing. Sometimes a reputation can be a heavy load to bear. Now, Jeff wasn't a bad kid or trouble-maker in school. In fact, he worked hard and was an outstanding student with the utmost respect for authority. But he's always had a mischievous side to him. Even in high school, he had a sly sense of humor and a crafty way that made pulling pranks one of his favorite pastimes. He wasn't trying to be disruptive, only to take a little edge off life.

Jeff still enjoys a good prank, even as a thirty-something quarterback in the NFL. In fact, one national football publication listed him number one on its list of "best locker room jokesters." Don't get the idea that Jeff doesn't take his work seriously. He does. It's *himself* that he doesn't take too seriously. Over the years he's learned how to lighten up when things get too heavy, how to have some fun when the dogs of drudgery start nipping at his heels. It's just his way of blowing off some steam.

An Early Start

Like his propensity to work hard and honor his commitments, Jeff's prankishness started back on the farm, where we kids were always pulling some kind of dirt on one another. We would hide one another's unattended dinner plates in the cupboards or toss one of our brother's shoes down the steps so we could get dressed and out to the chicken house to get our chores done first.

Jeff maintained his sense of humor throughout high school to the very end. One of the sweetest pranks he ever pulled took place on the night of his high school graduation valedictory speech.

There he stood at the podium—dressed in cap and gown and a shining example of what's good and right about America's youth—while the water guns he was hiding underneath his gown dripped on to the dais.

Word had gotten out to the administrators and teachers that these water pistols were the weapons of choice that year, so the principal issued an all-points bulletin, placing teachers at the top of the stage stairs for a search-and-seize operation. When Jeff arrived there, his biology teacher (knowing Jeff as well as the rest of us did) told him to lift up his gown. He did, revealing his machine gun and water bottles. *Busted!* Jeff thought. "OK, put your gown down and wait right here," the teacher said.

A few minutes later, the biology teacher returned with five or six other teachers. But instead of looking as if he were going to dress Jeff down, he was laughing. "Pull up your gown," the teacher said. Again, Jeff obeyed, expecting the wrath of his teachers to come down. Instead, they broke up laughing and told him, "Well, good luck!"

Jeff went about his business that night, armed for the fun that was sure to follow. By the way, his victims included several classmates, some teachers... and the principal.

Jeff never lost that puckish sense of humor or his craftiness in pulling pranks on his friends. In fact, he only got better at it as he moved through college and then to the National Football League.

Taking the Pranks to the Next Level

Jeff has a reputation around the NFL as being something of a straight-arrow. Everybody knows he's a Christian who grew up with a Mennonite family in Hollsopple, Pennsylvania. They know he's the kind of guy who considers a night at home playing with his kids a great time. But he's also known as a major league practical joker with a deft touch for pulling pranks on unsuspecting victims. That reputation followed him from the New York Giants to the Raiders and will most likely follow him wherever he goes.

Jeff has a repertoire of locker room gags that would do the Marx Brothers proud. Rich Stephens, a 300-pound offensive lineman with the Raiders and one of Jeff's victims said, "It gets to a point where you set your locker up, and if anything has moved, you know not to wear it. I'd hide my real shoes way under my locker and put a couple of dummy pairs out front so Hoss could get to them."

One of Jeff's favorite locker room pranks is to line the socks and gloves of teammates with a powder that turns into an indigo dye when it gets moist. The victim's feet and hands looked as if they have been dipped in a can of blue paint.

Howie Long and Jeff used to go round and round—strike, counter strike—pulling pranks on one another. On one occasion Howie discovered (too late) how painful and hot Atomic Balm can get when it's spread in an athletic supporter. He also discovered how hot Tobasco sauce can be when injected into fruit juice. On another occasion Jeff figured a way into Howie's hotel room right after the unsuspecting man left to catch the bus for the stadium. Seconds after Howie left, Jeff was in his room, then out to the bus— wearing Howie's favorite sweater. Howie glanced up as Jeff walked by, and noticing the sweater said, "Nice sweater, I have one that looks..." and then, after taking a closer look—at the sweater and at the grin on Jeff's face—realized his room had been raided.

Jeff and Phil Simms used to pick on one another quite a bit. It got pretty competitive. Jeff once got Simms with a prizewinner of a prank. He took Phil's car keys out of his pocket while he was in the shower, went out to the parking lot, got into his car, turned up the radio full blast and turned on the air conditioner. Then he put Vaseline on the windshield wipers and put them in the "on" position so that when the car was started they would spread the stuff all over. When Phil came out and turned on the ignition, everything started at once—the radio, the air conditioner, and the windshield wipers—and the Vaseline made such a mess he couldn't see through the glass.

(By the way, Phil still doesn't know who did it. He confronted Jeff about the prank, but Jeff managed to convince Phil it was Giants coach Johnny Parker who was responsible. Not one to wallow in remorse, Jeff then repeated the prank on Parker, implying that Simms did it. Now...you won't tell, will you?)

No one wants to be on Jeff's hit list. But don't think there weren't some paybacks! Jeff has been a victim of some beauties himself. It comes with the territory. Besides, that's half the fun of pulling pranks. He's learned, though, that finding out who was responsible for the prank isn't terribly difficult. Just wait for the truth to come out, he says, because pranksters are like terrorists—they can't wait to take credit for their work.

For example, one time Simms put redhot in Jeff's underwear when he was taking a shower after practice. But his plan backfired because Jeff noticed his underwear had been moved and could see that someone had laced them with redhot. Jeff didn't let on, though. He turned his back to Simms and slipped the extra pair of underwear he always carried (for just such an emergency) out of his bag and put them on the shelf in his locker. Then he went over to the sinks, brushed his teeth and combed his hair before he went back to get dressed. He could see a group of guys gathering at Simms' locker and knew they were all watching him to see what would happen next. He reached into his locker, got into his replacement underwear and started putting on his shirt in front of the mirror. As he sat down to put on his socks, he started fidgeting a little, as if something was bothering him. He sneaked a look at his buddies a couple of times and could see they were beginning to laugh, so he fidgeted a little more. He knew all the time that Simms was the redhot culprit, but he had to make sure he admitted to it. Therefore he finished dressing and kept up the itching act. Finally Phil walked over and said, very casually, "Something wrong with your underwear, Hoss?" Jeff said nothing, but instead reached into his bag for the tainted pair and threw them at him. Gotcha! He'd caught Simms red-handed!

Then there was the time Johnny Parker tried to get Jeff by putting a dead fish on the engine of his car, figuring that when Jeff started his car and the engine heated up, he'd get this really foul odor all through his car. The plan failed, though, because the fish smell was so strong *before* Jeff started the engine that he knew something was up. He lifted the hood and there was the scaley offender.

A Time for Levity

I don't want to give anybody the impression that Jeff's life in the NFL is one big joke, that he's nothing but a clown in a football uniform. No, Jeff realizes there is a time for joking around and a time for seriousness. Or, as Ecclesiastes 3:1 puts it, "There is a time for everything."

As a quarterback and leader in the game of football, Jeff knows how important it is to sense when the time is right for a little levity. But he also knows that for some players, joking around like that can be a detriment to the team. As he says, "If it becomes a distraction, then there's no place for it. Some guys can handle it without it becoming a distraction and others can't."

Some players just can't keep focused on their purpose when the fun begins. When the practical jokes start, they forget about their goals and the team's goals. And eventually it always shows up in their work and performance.

That is also true in other arenas of life. It can be especially true when it comes to our relationship with God. Life has a way of pulling pranks on us, causing us to become distracted from our mission, aim, and purpose. When that happens, it eventually shows up in our daily work habits and in how we approach our faith.

A prank that a Home Box Office photographer accidentally pulled on me illustrates what I mean.

Getting Blotted Out

Not long after the Giants Super Bowl XXV win, Jeff invited me to join him and Dad at the George Foreman-Evander Holyfield World Heavyweight Boxing Championship fight being held at Trump Plaza in Atlantic City, New Jersey. During a prefight dinner party, the HBO photographer took our pictures with Kevin Costner. Weeks later Jeff called and told me the photographs were supposedly being used for the covers of some tabloids and asked if I wanted a copy of one of the pictures.

"You bet!" I said. "I'll take one." But then Jeff began to chuckle as he told me about the call he had received from the photographer. Apparently the photographer didn't know who the guy in the middle of the picture was, so he inked him out. The guy was me.

Jeff and I both got a good laugh out of this incident. But you know what? The more we thought about that ink blot, the more we realized this is the way life is going to end for a lot of people who get distracted and carried away with the fun and frolic they pursue—or the pain and difficulty that pursues them. It will cause them to lose sight of their aim, mission, purpose, and goals, and leave a big, black hole in their souls.

That's one of the pranks life can play on us if we can't stay focused on who we are in Christ and what we are trying to accomplish in this world. We'll find our lives blotted out, just like I was in the HBO photograph. We need to be on our guard, too, because pranks don't come only in ugly packages. The things that help us to grow and benefit in many ways can also become pranks that life plays on us.

Pleasure, Pain, and Pride

Pleasure and pain can be great sources of motivation, but they can also become major distractions. The same is true of pride. All three can become pranks if they are not controlled.

Controlling Pleasure. Life on the road as a professional athlete is full of distracting, prank-provoking activity. Many of the young men who make a living playing professional sports get carried away with the pleasure—from sex and drugs to influence and power—that is freely offered someone who has the money and fame they enjoy. Many of them don't control their desire for pleasure and pleasure ends up controlling them. It takes discipline, self-control, and a solid, spiritual center of gravity to control our desire for pleasure.

Dealing with Pain. Pain comes in many shapes and sizes. It can be physical, emotional, mental, spiritual, or any combination thereof. It can be a positive thing in that it helps us know our limits or remind us when we've gone beyond them. It can become a negative when we let it distract us, become obsessed with it, or allow it to drive us to abusing remedies that only mask it.

Pain can be a great distraction for professional athletes. Physical pain has driven many of them to become addicted to pain-killing narcotics, giving them even worse pain. And the emotional pain of not starting or not accomplishing what they think they should has caused some athletes to use performance-enhancing drugs like steroids to give them an edge over their competition. Ignored or unmanaged pain felt in relationships often leads to the pain of separation and divorce.

Managing Pride. Pride is a subtle prank when it causes us to think more of ourselves than we should. That can happen to professional athletes when the money and fame and their accomplishments go to their heads. It seems as if everyone around pro athletes is encouraging them to become filled with pride. The constant media and fan attention is a heady experience for any young man, and Jeff is no exception. He is literally bombarded by fans seeking him out everywhere he goes. That kind of attention can cause professional athletes to have overinflated egos, to start thinking they are more important than they are just because people want to seek them out.

My own kids—Janna, Jared, and Bekah—saw some examples of this when I took them to the Super Bowl in Miami a few years ago. They were disappointed to see how full of pride these football heroes were as we dined and traveled with them to appearances and events.

The Prank of Wealth

Some people who live "ordinary" lives may look at the lives of professional athletes and think they have it made. The money, the fame, the opportunity to travel all look so appealing to those who work "real" jobs. But, believe it or not, life as a professional athlete can get old—especially to a Pennsylvania farm boy who lives to please his God and live out his commitment of love to his family.

Jeff would much rather be at home and love his wife, play with his kids, attend his own church, and visit with his neighbors than spend his time in hotels, meeting rooms, team dining rooms, and visiting locker rooms. To him, the latter obligations are just part of the life he must live as an NFL quarterback.

Life as a professional football player has been good to Jeff. He has much to be proud of, much to live for, much to get excited about, and much to be thankful for. But Jeff has kept his head about him despite the money and fame he has enjoyed. Sure, he enjoys the benefits of being a professional athlete, but he knows they can exact a price if they control him rather than him controlling them.

Jeff and I had a conversation recently during a trip on his four-wheeler though the back country behind his house in Morgantown. Eventually our conversation turned to money and stewardship. Jeff said with all sincerity, "You know, Ron, people may not believe it, but having a lot of money can be a curse."

I wouldn't know about that personally, but I know Jeff does. I believed him when he told me that, because he's not the first NFL player to say such a thing. Other players have told me that making a lot of money has not made them one bit happier.

That's the prank the National Football League has played on so many athletes. They come into the league believing the money and fame will make them happy, only to find out that if they were miserable before, money only makes them miserable *and* rich.

I wonder how many of us have fallen into the trap of thinking, *If only I had lots of money, I'd be happy* or *I'd be satisfied if only I could live in a really nice house* or *I'd finally be content if only I could afford a really expensive car?* Well, it's an old saying, but it's true: Money doesn't buy happiness! Neither do possessions. There's only one thing that gives us true, lasting joy and happiness, and that's knowing Jesus Christ as Lord and Savior.

I'm not about to suggest that Jeff hasn't enjoyed the fruits of his labor. His success in professional football has allowed him to enjoy a lifestyle that most of us couldn't imagine. But Jeff's money and possessions haven't changed Jeff Hostetler, the man. He has always enjoyed making other people happy and sharing what he has, and that hasn't changed. Jeff still loves to have his family come to his home in Morgantown for Fourth of July picnics. He loves sharing everything he has with us when we're there. We swim, boat, jet and water ski, play basketball and tennis, and hit tennis balls shot out of his ball machine.

Through Jeff's generosity we have gone places and met people we wouldn't have otherwise. Jeff has helped get us tickets for the Super Bowl and all the other special events that take place during this extraordinary weekend. One of our most memorable experiences occurred in Minneapolis, Minnesota, backstage of the auditorium from which Turner Television was broadcasting during its Super Bowl special. We sat at a table with syndicated columnist Andy Rooney, talking about dairy cows and milk, while other celebrities and sports stars milled about. One of my brothers-in-law looked like a kid at an Easter egg hunt as he scurried about, getting autographs and taking pictures.

And Jeff made it all possible. That's the kind of person he is. To him, the money and possessions that accompany professional football mean nothing if he can't share them with the ones he loves.

Meeting the Demands of Stardom

With the fame and money come monumental demands for Jeff's time and financial resources. As much as Jeff would like to live up to the expectations of others, it's physically and emotionally impossible for him to do it.

Many people approach Jeff to ask for money for their cause or charity. I've seen letters to him from all over the world asking for money. Although many of the requests are sincere and heartfelt, it's hard to tell who's making up a story or singing a real song of misfortune. For this reason, our family is very protective of Jeff. He's been most gracious in granting some personal favors and requests, but someone in Jeff's position can quickly feel taken advantage of, and we try to keep that from happening.

Still the Jeff We Knew

Jeff has come a long way. He's countered some of the biggest pranks life can throw at him with some of his own. And although Jeff's lifestyle has changed, his values haven't. Nor has his character. He's still the same Jeff we've always known, only he's more mature in his faith and character. He's worked hard to keep life's pranks from taking his focus off what God always intended him to be: a humble servant of God.

Jeff's success in the National Football League has taken him places he never dreamed of going when he was growing up. But when it comes to peace, contentment, happiness, and fulfillment, Jeff knows there's no place like home. That's why he works hard at keeping a mental picture of life at the end of the lane where he grew up, where the mailbox used to read, "Dolly's Delight Farm, R.D.#1, Hollsopple."

CHAPTER NINE

A GAME OF FLINCH:
DEALING WITH INJURIES

I f you've ever watched an NFL quarterback standing in the pocket with arm cocked, scanning for a receiver while a half-ton of human steamrollers look to separate him from the ball (and maybe from consciousness), you might wonder how he keeps his cool. Part of what makes an NFL quarterback successful is his poise, courage, and toughness, all under intense fire.

Jeff Hostetler learned early in his football career the value of being able to stand tall in the pocket while a defensive team full of very large, very athletic men come crashing in around him from all angles. That's not something every quarterback can learn and Jeff had to go through his time of adjustment during the early years of his NFL career. But as with so many things, Jeff had begun learning those things while growing up on the farm.

Testing our mettle was a common practice for the Hostetler boys and we certainly weren't at a loss when it came to thinking of ways to do it. One game of courage we found particularly fun was called "flinch." It was a simple game, really. All we needed was a football and steady nerves.

We'd lie on our backs, side-by-side or in a circle, with our heads centered toward the middle like spokes on a wheel. We'd then take turns tossing up a football, the object being to put the right amount of arc and height on the throw so the ball would land squarely on somebody's face.

Not so hard, you think? You're right—except that our game had a catch: We weren't allowed to catch or move out of the way of the descending football. We couldn't so much as flinch, and if anyone moved to escape the impact, he would get rocked with right-handers from the other players.

We spent hours on end working to get the perfect strike, and we laughed especially hard when someone tossed a self-inflicted bomb. Call it poise under pressure or just plain stupidity, but there we'd lay, like Spartans taking hits on our noses, lips, foreheads, and other outlying areas—just to prove ourselves tough and durable.

But you know what? Playing flinch was fun! Of course, trying to explain away fat lips and facial bruises to our friends at school was an impossibility, but we had some of our best times as kids playing this game.

Did it help make us tough? Perhaps. Should it have knocked some sense into us? Probably. But we really didn't think about those things back then; we were just having a good time.

While I don't know if our sadistic little game helped Jeff's quarterbacking skills a great deal, I can't help but think it prepared him for what was ahead in the violent world of the National Football League.

Playing Flinch in the NFL

I don't know how many times I've nervously watched as Jeff stood in the pocket, waiting till the last second to deliver a pass, knowing the pain that would follow. It amazes me how he can be so calm, knowing what's going on around him, that he is one badly placed hit away from a season- or career-ending injury.

It always hurts to see my brother injured when he's hit. But I know, as does Jeff, that injuries are a part of the game.

In 1993 and 1994 those injuries came in the form of concussions, including one against the Steelers in which he left the game seeing flashing lights. While then-Raiders Coach Art Shell was leery of putting Jeff back in the game, he respected his quarterback's toughness and willingness to come back after taking a pounding.

Jeff's 1995 season with the Raiders was filled with injuries and ended with shoulder surgery to repair a torn rotator cuff in his left (nonthrowing) shoulder after absorbing a painful hit by Chad Hennings in a game against the Dallas Cowboys. Hennings, an outspoken Christian and a true gentleman who would never try to hurt anybody, felt bad about the injury. Jeff didn't know that the injury actually occurred a couple of games before that in New York playing against his old team, the Giants.

On a third-and-long play, Jeff scrambled to secure a first down and keep a winning drive alive. Unable to soften his fall with his left hand—he had broken that in three places the week before—he hit the hard, cold, unyielding turf shoulder first and felt a snap and searing pain. The impact of the fall ripped his shoulder from its socket like a drumstick being pulled from a turkey on Thanksgiving Day. Despite the excruciating pain, Jeff stayed in the game and helped lead the Raiders to a 17-13 win. But the damage had been done. Jeff couldn't even dress himself in the locker room afterward and our brother Doug had to help him put on his shirt and coat and tie his shoes.

This had been his fourth injury in four straight weeks, a disturbing trend for a team that needed a healthy quarterback to have any chance to get to the Super Bowl. Jeff's first injury that season was a compression fracture of his windpipe in Denver on an ABC Monday night game, when he was struck in the neck while the Broncos were returning a fumble.

Jeff stayed in the game until the third quarter, but the swelling and pain got so bad he couldn't call the plays or audible at the line of scrimmage. Soon after that, he started having trouble breathing. X-rays taken in the locker room afterward confirmed a serious injury and he was taken to the hospital and advised to stay the night for close observation. He was glad he did, as the doctor later told him he could have died on the plane trip home without sufficient medical equipment or treatment.

The injury made it difficult to swallow and Jeff was put on a one-week diet of soup and liquids. He missed the Raiders' next game, a home date with the Indianapolis Colts, but returned to practice on the following Wednesday and Thursday. He wasn't 100 percent yet, but he was getting close to being ready to play.

Jeff didn't have much time to heal before sustaining another injury. He returned against Cincinnati and cracked several bones in his left hand when it was sandwiched between the helmets and shoulder pads of a couple of defensive linemen. X-rays revealed shattered bones and displaced cartilage. On top of that, the tip of one of his fingers on his throwing hand was fractured, causing it to lean over. It wouldn't stand up on its own so doctors had to drill into the bone and put a pin in the finger. The following week in practice, Jeff uncovered the bandage to see why the tip of his finger was so sharp. It turned out the pin had worked its way up out of the bone and through his flesh. The doctor took a pair of pliers and pushed it back down into the bone. We all cringed when Jeff told us about it.

By the time the 1995 season ended, Jeff had missed all of five games and parts of four others due to his assorted injuries. The Raiders struggled, too, finishing 8-8 and out of the American Football Conference playoffs. That hurt after an impressive 8-2 start.

Sticking with It

Although 1995 was a tough season from the injury standpoint, Jeff never flinched from his responsibilities. As his injuries mounted, he didn't shy away from the pain, the rehabilitation, the practice, or his duties. He stood his ground and repeatedly worked his way back.

Playing through pain and standing firm under pressure is one of the things that makes a quarterback a great leader, and Jeff is just that kind of quarterback. His example inspires the ten men around him to stand their ground, especially his linemen.

Raider offensive guard Steve Wisniewski once said of Jeff: "To his own fault sometimes, he'll step up and hold the ball until that receiver breaks or until something opens up. You don't see him throwing out of bounds that often, getting the happy feet you hear about in the NFL. He'll stand in there and take his shot. Sometimes we'll tell him, 'Throw the ball away if it's not there, Hoss. Don't take any more hits.' But that's not his style."

Managing Pain

National Football League players learn quickly that they've got to play through pain. Pain is part of football and players need to be able to differentiate between pain and injury.

While NFL players and coaches need to make distinctions between pain and injury, sometimes that isn't easy to do. Pressure to perform can cause players to cross the line between what is safe for them and what helps their teams or careers.

There's an old saying in the NFL about injured players spending time in the whirlpool bath: "You can't help the club in the tub." Professional football players have to recover, and recover quickly, from their injuries. Standing in the gap for these iron men is an arsenal of drugs, high-tech protective devices, and surgical procedures.

Jeff knows a lot about these things. He used most of the tried-and-true methods of fighting pain, including: heat treatments for muscle injuries; cold sprays and ice packs for ankles, knees, hands, and shoulders; non-steroidal anti-inflammatory drugs for injured ligaments and joints; non-narcotic painkillers for playing with bruised bones and fractures; electrical stimulators to speed up healing of muscle tears; special padding to shield fractured bones; flexible braces to support sprained knees; aggressive surgical procedures to fix fractures; and anesthetic injections to mask pain and postpone surgery.

This list of treatments alone is enough to make anyone flinch, but in the world of the National Football League, resting an injury or avoiding pain often is not an option. Whether they're stars or not, players do not want to miss games and they will push the limits of endurance to stay in, often out of fear that someone else will take their place.

Medical advice is based on standards of a different kind in the NFL and you can be certain most men who are left standing at the end of a season had played their final game with bruises, sprains and strains that would send most grown men to the doctor's office.

Enduring the Recovery

Although the surgery to repair Jeff's shoulder went well, his doctor told Jeff it was the worst of its kind he had ever seen. Everything around the joint was either gone or torn to shreds. Even the large muscle that stretched around the torso to his back had been torn.

It's hard for somebody who hasn't gone through this kind of injury and recovery to understand what Jeff had to tolerate. Not only did he have to go through the surgery itself, but he also had to endure a long, grueling rehabilitation. Jeff said it was the most painful thing he'd ever experienced. He couldn't sleep for weeks and the medication for pain didn't help much, if at all.

As you might guess, the experience turned Jeff into something of a walking physician's desk reference. Jeff wanted to understand everything that was being done for him, from the medication he was taking and its effects to the different kinds of surgical techniques that could be performed.

Jeff took these things very seriously because his body isn't just his livelihood; it is also the temple of the Lord. Therefore he worked hard at understanding how it worked.

Jeff had learned from his experience with his son Jason (and from Mom) that you need to ask questions, check references, and get second and third opinions. He took Mom's words seriously, because Mom knew all about what it was like to live with pain.

Turning to the Great Physician

Like Jeff, Mom had been a victim of pain's arbitrary and capricious nature. It didn't seem fair to us that Mom would have to suffer like she did, but through her suffering, Mom brought glory to God…and taught us an important lesson about what to do when sickness or injury hits for no apparent reason.

Mom could have used her pain as an excuse to give up and to begin feeling sorry for herself. But that wasn't the way of this remarkable woman. Instead of sitting in the corner wallowing in self-pity, Mom called on the Great Physician for help.

Mom had the kind of faith in God that gave her the assurance that no matter what kind of suffering she had to endure, no matter what kind of injustice came her way, she could persevere through it with the help of her Lord and Savior. Even though she never was able to completely cast off the troubling companion of pain, she found relief in the hands of the Lord's grace.

Mom used to tell us how much she looked forward to going home to heaven so she could get a new body. It made us sad to hear her say this because we loved our mom and wanted her to stay here with us, but at the same time, we knew what she meant. We knew that part of what got Mom through the tough times was her faith that someday she would stand before her heavenly Father in a new body, a body that would never feel pain or sickness or aging.

Mom's example taught all of us how to endure and stay the course when injuries or illness came into our lives. Our brothers Todd and Doug both endured and stayed the course when injuries cut short their college sports careers and any chances they had of professional ones. I did, too.

After his surgery, Jeff was determined to pass pain's test. Over the days, weeks, and months that followed, he worked his way back, just as he had from all his other injuries.

Jeff learned a lot through that experience. He learned to be thankful for the wonderful, marvelous, workings of medicine and the divinely created human body it is designed to help. But more importantly, Jeff learned something about the nature of God when we are suffering. God does not disappear when we are in pain; it is then that He most reaches down to comfort and encourage us. Because of that, Jeff was able to endure his pain, knowing that God cared and would be there to comfort him when Jeff turned to Him for help.

Beyond Our Control

A song titled "Heads or Tails" contains a verse that says, "Sometimes we try to blaze our own trail, we make our plans in every detail, it's easy to think that we're in control but God only knows where your life will go."

There's so much truth in those words. As much as we may struggle with it, only God knows what lies ahead for us. Not only does He know what's ahead, He's *in control* of what happens to His children. And the sooner we learn that He's in control, the sooner we can be at peace with the things that are beyond our control.

The bottom line is, there's no way to completely control things like injuries. Jeff had done everything he could to prevent his injuries, but they were ultimately out of his control. As random and unjust as injuries may seem to be, they are a part of life.

In a way, the injuries were a lot like the emotional pain Jeff felt early in his career when he wasn't playing. He knew he could be a quality NFL quarterback, but there was nothing he could do about his coach's decision about whom to play. Jeff could plan, prepare, and persevere in order to make it in the NFL, but there was nothing he could do to control the circumstances that would come his way.

But there was one thing Jeff could control: his response to the situation, his attitude. Like all of us, Jeff could have chosen to feel sorry for himself and sulk when things didn't go his way. He could have turned away from God and back to his own way of soothing the pain. But he didn't. Instead he chose to respond positively and responsibly to his newest challenge.

As children of a loving, concerned God, each of us has this choice. We can let the negative things that happen destroy our hope and confidence, or we can turn tragedy into triumph by letting God have our ashes when lightning strikes.

God loves it when His children bring their injuries, their hurts, and their injustices before Him. At the moments of our greatest weakness, at the times of our worst injuries and hurts, God shows and proves Himself more than strong enough to bring us up from the ashes of pain and despair. But we have to do our part by acknowledging and calling upon Him for help.

A Final Thought

Injuries come into everyone's life, but none of us have to play the "If Only" game. Don't punish yourself by saying things like, "If only I would have stretched better" or "If only I had worked a little harder" or "If only I had done it differently."

"If Only" thinking not only doesn't help, it is downright destructive. It keeps you locked into the past and focused on your injury.

God has a way of recycling damaged goods and turning tragedies into opportunities. Just remember, *"The worst thing that ever happens to you, might be the best thing that ever happens to you—if you don't let it get the best of you."*

Jeff hasn't let injuries get the best of him, even though they've done their worst to knock him out of the game he loves. In a real sense, they never had a chance. A boy who grows up playing flinch isn't about to be bothered by a little bout with pain.

CHAPTER TEN

LASTING LESSONS FROM MOM:
DEMONSTRATIONS OF FAITH AND LOVE

J ust six weeks after he led the New York Giants to a win in Super Bowl XXV, Jeff received a call he never wanted to get. He was returning to Washington D.C. after doing an autograph card show in Newark when an airline official at the terminal gave him a message to call Vicky, who was staying at our brother Doug's house in Washington while Jeff was away. Worried that it might be another problem with Jason, Jeff called her right away. Vicky quickly assured him that Jason was fine, but then she delivered the news:

Jeff's mother had just died.

The news hit Jeff like a sledgehammer. It just didn't seem real that the woman who had done so much for him, who had given so much to shape his life, was gone. He was in shock. He boarded the plane for Washington and took what he later called "the slowest and saddest" trip he'd ever known. Todd and Doug met him at the airport and he was glad they did. It was time to huddle together.

When Jeff walked through the door of the old farmhouse, our eyes met and so did our breaking hearts. We hugged each other while tears of sadness worked hard to wash away the overwhelming grief that washed over our souls.

We knew Mom was in a far better place now, that she was in the presence of our heavenly Father with a new, glorified body. And we knew that someday we'd see Mom again, no longer troubled by the pain that had racked her body for all those years. But we knew something else with equal certainty: We were going to miss her.

Mom was a wonderful, special woman in so many ways. Not only did she give us life, she bequeathed to all of us a spiritual and emotional grounding that we live with to this day. But no longer would she be there for us to confide in. No longer would she be there to offer tips and suggestions on how to raise and discipline our kids or maximize marriage and resolve conflict. There would be no more phone calls of counsel and encouragement. No more cards to inspire or Bible verses to memorize or books to read or tapes to listen to. No more words of praise or notes of encouragement in the mail. No more prayers of faith that seemed to move mountains. No more soprano solos that shook the heavens.

No more Mom.

We knew we would miss all those things. We would miss Mom more than she could know.

Drawing Close to One Another

The whole extended family gathered at the old Hostetler farmhouse. This wasn't a first; we'd all met there many times before over the years. After leaving home, we all continued to meet there for Christmas, Thanksgiving, Easter, and Fourth of July celebrations. Mom made it a point that she wanted everyone home—no excuses. And we were all happy to comply.

But it was different this time. Instead of the normal laughter and enthusiasm that marked such gatherings, today there was only low murmuring and drawn faces. Each of us seemed locked in our own world of unattached thoughts, memory flashes, and unanswered questions.

We all knew Mom had been sick and in pain, but we also knew her as a woman with unquenchable strength and perseverance. Even with the searing pain from her arthritis and back problems, Mom had much to live for. And she had hung in there, long enough to make the trip to Tampa to watch her son play in the game of his life in the Super Bowl. Mom was sick and in pain before going to the Super Bowl and Jeff had tried talking her into entering the hospital. But she was adamant: She was going to the Super Bowl and that was that. Little did any of us know it would be the last game she would ever attend.

The next forty-eight hours with the family seemed unreal as we all walked around in a fog of sadness. It just didn't seem possible that Mom was really gone. Any moment now we should hear Mom's familiar call to the supper table and we'd all gather around to sing our prayer. But the evidence was everywhere. The flowers, the folks coming and going with quiet words of consolation, the tear-stained faces of Mom's grieving children. They all told the same story.

Yet even in her passing, Mom drove home to us the lessons that she had taught us all our lives—lessons about faith, devotion to God and to family, and passing that faith on to those we love.

Mom's Diary

Shortly after her death, our sisters found Mom's diary. As Jeff and I sat in the family room and opened it, we listened intently once again to the words of the special woman who had helped guide our lives. We pored over page after page of Mom's longings, heartaches, joys, tribulations, and convictions. It was amazing to read the record Mom left behind, especially when she was communicating directly with her heavenly Father. She talked with God on a heart-to-heart basis, as with a trusted friend. Like the psalmist David, she hid nothing from God as she expressed her innermost thoughts, emotions, and desires. Seeing that in the pages of this book made her even more of a role model to us than she had been before.

Mom had known a lot of suffering and sadness in her life. But despite family tragedies and a body racked with almost perpetual pain, her faith in God remained steadfast. Somehow, even in the darkest moments, Mom knew how to glimpse the pinpoint of God's light in the distance. Mom just kept trusting in God's faithfulness. In every accident, every trial, and every disaster, Mom somehow saw God's hand of providence. She clung to His promises with a hope that never quit...and she had taught her seven children to do the same.

Reading her diary reminded us of the words Mom stitched to our hearts every morning as each of us left the house: "Remember who you are and Whose you are." And it reminded us of what she would say when we faced discouragement or confusion: "God has a very special plan for your life."

"How many times," Jeff reflected, "did I need to hear those words! Times when it seemed that God had either discarded me or forgotten any special plan He might have once had for my life."

Mom was always there when we needed to hear such words. That's something none of us will ever forget about her.

A Recorded Miracle

As we continued to read in Mom's diary of her faith in God and love for Him and of her devotion for her children, we came across an amazing passage that recorded a special moment in Jeff's life. It concerned the 1990 NFC championship game in San Francisco when Jeff was seemingly knocked out of the game with a knee injury.

We remembered the incident well. Jeff was focusing on his wide receivers downfield when, suddenly, out of the corner of his eye, he glimpsed a flash of red and gold. Of course, Jeff wanted to step out of harm's way, but it was too late. Former Giant-turned-49er Jim Burt crashed into his leg with the full force of a freight train, knocking him to the turf in agonizing pain.

As I sat from my perch in the stands with my son Jared, I remember thinking with absolute certainty that it was all over for Jeff that season. Jeff later said he knew it was over, too. Thunderbolts of pain shot up his leg. As he lay on the ground, writhing in pain, Jeff was certain he was done. In a moment's time, his hopes of leading his team to the Super Bowl had vanished.

Well, not quite! Jeff might be down and out, but not Mom. Oh, she had been too sick to make the trip to the West Coast, but she was with Jeff anyway, watching on television and praying Jeff through his pain and disappointment.

And she asked God for a miracle.

We turned to the page in Mom's diary where she had been taking notes on the game. She had made painstaking records of her son's statistics, recorded what announcers said about him, and translated her emotions during every key moment in the game. Now, as she watched her son lie on the ground in agony, she recorded the depths of her prayers to God. And her words described a miracle.

We're sure Mom prayed out loud as she wrote. In short, emotion-filled sentences, she asked God to take away Jeff's pain, to stoop down and heal her son and let him finish the game he had waited so many years to play. Three thousand miles away in San Francisco, Jeff lay on the field while the trainers gathered around him. The pain and disappointment he felt were brutal. But then, something incredible happened.

"Suddenly, out of nowhere, everything just stopped," Jeff recalls. "The pain and the fear faded inexplicably. It was unbelievable. I felt a calming, peaceful sensation that started from my head and went down through my leg to my toes. I still can't explain it. One moment I was in total pain, and then suddenly I knew everything was OK. I knew I could get up."

And he did. Of course everybody, especially Coach Parcells, was worried. Three times he asked Jeff, "Hoss, can you go back in?" Twice Jeff answered, "Yeah, I can go." The third time, Jeff said with certainty, "Bill, I'm going!" And he did, too, leading the Giants downfield for Matt Bahr's field goal for the winning points and a trip to Super Bowl XXV.

Only when we read Mom's diary did we realize fully what had taken place. Jeff just shook his head in wonder. "I never knew," he mumbled as tears welled up in his eyes. Reading this account in Mom's diary was a new revelation. Until that moment, Jeff didn't realize that what lay behind his incredible recovery at Candlestick Park was the believing prayers of a mother who loved her boy beyond anything he could understand. Reading Mom's account of what happened that day in San Francisco welded to our minds the importance of faith, of believing that God truly has a plan to glorify Himself in our lives and do what is best for us.

Looking over his long and difficult road through the lens of Mom's words, Jeff could see how God had planned all along to turn all his trials into triumph. He could see that God never deserted him and Vicky during their struggle with Jason's illness. Even when God seemed far away, even when Jeff wanted to turn away from Him in anger, the Father was right there, ready to comfort Jeff and Vicky and work His will for their lives.

Jeff knows now that God was right there with him, teaching him valuable life lessons and working His perfect will in his life during all those frustrating years standing on the sidelines with the New York Giants. As we read Mom's diary, we could just hear her words as if she were standing right there with us: "God has a plan for your life. Just because things don't go your way doesn't mean that plan has changed."

As He did with Mom with her tragedies and illnesses, with Dad and his setbacks on the farm, with Jason and his death-defying fight, God has allowed trials into Jeff's life to forge the inner steel structure of character and faith. That's the powerful lesson from Mom's diary.

Words of Devotion

Reading Mom's diary gave us a look into the heart of the woman who loved us with an unyielding devotion, who taught us in words and actions what love and commitment for God and for her family really mean. Mom and Dad had always taught us how important it was for us to be devoted to one another through anything and everything. And those lessons of love sank in. Although we may have fought among ourselves like all brothers and sisters do, there was no questioning our devotion to one another.

That was especially evident when somebody outside our family picked a fight with one of us. Every single one would come charging to the rescue whenever that happened. It was like that for the boys in all situations, but most memorably on the gridiron, basketball court, and baseball diamond. One moment we could be arguing and fighting among ourselves during a game, and the next moment we could be defending each other from our opponents like a raging grizzly bear.

It's still like that. I remember an incident at Giants Stadium when Jeff returned as a Raider to play his old team. As I and my son sat there with Jon Miller, senior vice president of programming for NBC, and his two boys, we began to become annoyed and offended by a couple of young men who were taking turns calling Jeff names and talking about him using obnoxious, profane language. It soon got to the point where I'd heard enough. As Popeye used to say, "I can stand what I stands, but I can't stands no more!" I launched a direct, verbal strike of my own, telling them in no uncertain terms to button their lips.

I know! I know! That was probably a stupid thing to do, but there was no way I was going to let these guys talk about my brother like that. Sure enough, things got a little heated between me and these guys. In the nick of time Jon stood up and stepped in with a threat to have them thrown out of the stadium if they kept up their taunts. And you know what? It worked! After that, if they said anything, they kept it to themselves.

Later on in the parking lot, while all of us savored a Raiders win over the Giants—and our personal victory over their two most obnoxious fans—I put my arm around Jon and thanked him for jumping in to help me. At that moment, it was as if he had joined the Hostetler boys. We walked to our cars with our kids in tow, feeling the warm afterglow of demonstrated commitment and support.

Yet that wasn't the end of it. Jon later wrote us a letter describing how meeting the Hostetler clan had impacted him:

Dear Guys:
It isn't often I put pen to paper, but this weekend was so special in so many ways that I felt compelled to write all of you.

We all knew what this game meant not only to Jeff, but to all of us, and I wanted to share something with you that puts the entire weekend into perspective.

In the car on the way home from the game last evening after all the celebration, fun, and cold had passed, Jeffrey, my 10-year-old, said from out of the blue, "Dad, there sure is a lot of love in the Hostetler family." For a moment, I couldn't speak... "Out of the mouths of babes" comes some of the truest sentiments. He is not only observant, he is right on target.

The three most important things in life are family, faith, and friends, and you have shared all of that with each other and with our family. The example you set and the way you support and cherish each other is truly remarkable. Your relationship serves as an inspiration to me and my boys. (Ron, I think you know that had that guy in front of you kept going, we were all going to find ourselves in the slammer! Just ask Todd!)

You all have something very extraordinary here—thanks for letting me be a small part of it.

Jon

That letter reminded us how grateful we are for Mom's example of devotion and love. It reminded us why that devotion is so important: It bonds people together and makes them willing to lay down everything they have, even their lives, for the sake of one another. That's the kind of love Mom taught us as she gave us everything she had to mold us into the kind of people we are today.

Saying Goodbye

We felt that same kind of devotion toward Mom. I'll never forget how Jeff said goodbye to Mom at her funeral. It was his last act of devotion toward her. With tears in his eyes, Jeff handed me a small clump of dandelions to place in Mom's hands.

You see, dandelions were a symbol of Jeff's devotion to Mom. As a toddler, he frequently went out into the fields and picked them for her with his chubby, grubby little paws, greatly anticipating the sunny smile and warm embrace that would follow when he brought them to her. Then he would watch as she carefully placed them in a vase so the world could see his tokens of love.

On that day, Mom couldn't reach out and accept Jeff's symbol of devotion. Twenty-nine years after giving birth to a future Super Bowl hero, Mom was gone. Her eyes, her hands, her feet, her voice, all slumbered in silent stillness as the funeral director closed her coffin, entombing the small clump of flowers that would forever symbolize Jeff's undying, unyielding love and affection for the woman who had been his first love, whose hands had nurtured, cared for, and lovingly held him.

Passing on a Legacy

When Mom passed on, she left with her children memories and lessons of faith and devotion about what it means to love. She also showed us the importance of leaving something of lasting significance behind for our children. Jeff has something he will leave for his three boys: the value of hard work, faith, and perseverance.

When Jeff is gone, he will have two Super Bowl rings to leave his sons. Perhaps the rings will remind them of their dad, of watching him play on those glorious Sunday afternoons. But what Jeff wants them to remember most from those rings is not so much his statistics or even his Super Bowl win, but the story behind them.

He wants them to remember his work ethic, how Mom and Dad and his coaches and teachers and brothers and sisters all challenged him to work hard, work well, and work to God's glory. He wants them to remember how his works were tested by fire and how to stand firm without flinching.

He wants them to remember the ways and means in which God worked in his life, how He taught him patience, perseverance, and hard work when his NFL career seemed dead. And he wants them to remember how God worked a miracle for him and Vicky in the life of their firstborn son.

He wants his boys to remember that God's goal for them is to work out their faith by working through difficulties, as He works in them His character and nature. He wants them to learn about God's glorious, working ways in order to discover what works when life doesn't. And he wants them to never forget that they are His workmanship and that all His work is good.

Jeff wants his boys to know they were created in Christ Jesus to do good works, and he wants them to remember to keep their eyes focused on the greater works that God prepared them for in advance—like works of service, works of faith, and works of love.

Jeff wants them to remember that it takes work to reap the rewards, that it takes sweat and suffering and sometimes sorrow to secure success.

And, most of all, he wants them to remember the example of Jesus Christ, who sweat drops of blood in the Garden of Gethsemane as He agonized over the work before Him, then endured the cross for our sakes, making salvation possible for us.

This is the "inside stuff" Jeff wants to impart to his sons' hearts, minds, and souls. This is the stuff winning legacies are made of. It's his challenge to them.

And to you.

What's Ahead?

What lies ahead for Jeff is uncertain. He wants to fulfill the remaining years left on his contract with the Raiders, but with a new coach and another quarterback coming in, age creeping up, and injuries taking longer to heal, only the Lord knows what lies ahead for him and his family. But that's OK with Jeff. He's been here before and he knows God is in control and has his best interests in mind.

Jeff would like to play a few more seasons in the NFL, be it with the Raiders or with someone else. Either way, he knows God is in control and has a plan. And when his days of playing are over, he would like to become more personally involved with the Hoss Foundation he started several years back. Perhaps he will put to work his education as a certified financial planner, writing financial investments for clients.

Most of all, he will work at growing stronger in his commitment to the Lord and in his covenant relationship to Vicky. He will also enjoy watching his boys take on the world like he once did. He will watch them grow up and play football in the backyard. He will break up their fights and discipline them and tell them to go figure it out for themselves when they get into nasty scrapes.

He will tell them God has a perfect plan for their lives, even when that plan appears elusive. He will pray for them, play with them, and stand with them until some brown-eyed beauty comes along to steal their hearts, like their mother once did with him. He will walk them through every injury, every heartbreak, and every trial that comes their way, reminding them of God's hand and provision when they feel like quitting.

Through it all, he and Vicky will ask God for the grace and wisdom they will need to be the kind of parents God wants them to be.

Dad will laugh and encourage them, remembering the days when he and Mom would say, "You just wait till you have kids." And Mom, precious Mom, will just watch and smile—from heaven.

A JEFF HOSTETLER PROFILE

Personal

- Born April 22, 1961.
- Grew up in Hollsopple, Pennsylvania. One of seven children born to Norman Jr. and Dolly Hostetler. Three brothers: Ron, Norman Douglas, Jon Todd. Three sisters: Gloria Dawn, Cheryl Joy, Lori Jeanne.
- Married in 1984 to Vicky, daughter of college coach Don Nehlen. Three sons: Jason, Justin, and Tyler.
- Lives in Morgantown, West Virginia, with wife and sons.
- Hobbies include boating, other water sports, and landscaping.
- Founder of the Hoss Foundation, a nonprofit ministry to help people wishing to adopt children and to meet the financial needs of children with handicaps.

In High School

- Four-sport star at Conemaugh Township High School in Davidsville, Pennsylvania.
- Scholastic All-America linebacker during senior season.
- One-thousand-yard rusher as running back during senior season after switching from quarterback position. Earned player of the year honors from the Southern Alleghenies Football Coaches Association.
- *Parade* magazine All-America linebacker his senior season.
- All-League forward in basketball, sprinter in track, and All-State infielder in baseball.
- Class valedictorian for Conemaugh Township class of 1979.

In College

•Attended Penn State University his freshman and sophomore years and played football for Joe Paterno's Nittany Lions both years before transferring to West Virginia.

•All-America quarterback as junior and senior after leading West Virginia to consecutive 9-3 seasons, compiling 4,055 passing yards on 290 completions with twenty-four touchdowns.

•ABC Player of the Week as junior after completing seventeen passes for 321 yards and four touchdowns during win over Oklahoma University.

•Helped lead Mountaineers to Gator Bowl appearance during junior year and Hall of Fame Bowl berth during senior season.

•Placed fourth in Heisman Trophy vote his senior year.

•Played in Hula Bowl and Japan Bowl after senior season.

•Finance major in college.

•Academic All-American as senior.

•One of eleven scholar athletes honored by National Football Foundation Hall of Fame.

•Nominated for Rhodes Scholarship.

An NFL Scouting Report

•A six-foot-three-inch, 215-pound quarterback.

•Played with New York Giants from 1984 to 1992 after being drafted in third round of 1984 college draft.

•Saw action in all sixteen games in 1988 with one start late in season against New Orleans. Completed sixteen of twenty-nine passes for 244 yards and one touchdown, an eighty-five-yarder for New York's longest pass completion of '88.

•Saw action in all sixteen games in 1989 as reserve and holder on place kicks with one start against Phoenix, when he completed twenty of thirty-nine passes for 294 yards and three touchdowns.

•In 1990, active for all sixteen league games for New York as backup quarterback and holder on place kicks. Replaced injured starter in week fourteen and directed club to pair of wins to clinch NFC East title, then led Giants to three straight playoff wins culminating in Super Bowl XXV victory over Buffalo, turning in a twenty of thirty-two, 222-yard, one-touchdown performance.

•Started twelve games for Giants in '91 and set club record for single-season completion percentage at 62.8 on 179 of 285 passes for 2,032 yards and five touchdowns. Also set Giants single-game completion percentage record of 82.3 with a twenty-eight of thirty-four passes, 368-yard performance against Dallas. Interception percentage of 1.4 was lowest in NFL for 1991.

•Signed by Raiders as unrestricted free agent in March 1993.

•With 3,242 yards passing in 1993, became only third quarterback in Raider history to pass for more than three thousand yards in a single season.

•Set Raider single-season record for rushing touchdowns by quarterback with five, including one in each of four straight games (against Cincinnati, Buffalo, Seattle, and Tampa Bay) in 1993.

•AFC Offensive Player of the Week after completing Raider record fifteen passes in a row against Minnesota on twenty-three of twenty-seven passes in 1993 season.

•Set Raider single-game record with career-high 424 passing yards against San Diego in 1993.

•Threw for 310 yards, three touchdowns, completing twenty-five of forty-one passes, including game-tying four-yard touchdown pass to Alexander Wright in closing seconds of league season finale versus Denver. The play tied the score and sent the game into overtime, which the Raiders won and advanced to host playoff contest against Broncos in 1993.

•Started all sixteen league games at quarterback for Raiders in 1994 and passed for 3,334 yards, second-highest single-season total in Raider history. Completed 263 of 454 passes with twenty touchdowns that season, all career highs.

•Passed for 338 yards, four touchdowns, completing twenty-one of thirty-three passes on September 18, 1994, at Denver.

•Had 310 yards, three touchdowns on twenty-two of twenty-eight passes on November 20, 1994, against New Orleans.

•Passed for 319 yards and two touchdowns, including a seventy-six-yarder to Alexander Wright, on twenty-two of twenty-nine completions December 5, 1994, game at San Diego.

•Completion percentage of 57.2 over Raider career is second-best in team history.

•In thirty-one games as a Raider, has thrown for 6,576 yards to rank eighth in team career passing yardage, completing 499 of 873 passes with thirty-four touchdowns over that span.

•Has played in 106 league contests in ten NFL seasons through 1996.